A CHILD'S WORLD

A CHILD'S WORLD

A unique insight into how children think

ver

tting

Falkirk Council

headline

Dedicated to Saxon, Roman and Sapphire

*Dr Sarah Brewer is the author of over
25 books, including:*

Planning a Baby?

The Complete Book of Men's Health

Super Baby

I Want To Have A Baby?

Increase Your Sex Drive

Pregnancy – The Natural Way

Detox Yourself

The Ultimate Stressbuster

First published in 2001
by HEADLINE BOOK PUBLISHING

First published in paperback in 2002
by HEADLINE BOOK PUBLISHING

10 9 8 7 6 5 4 3 2 1

ISBN 0 7472 51185

Text design by Isobel Gillan

A CHILD'S WORLD
A Wall to Wall production for Channel 4 and
The Learning Channel in association with
Granada International
Series producer: Louise Rota
Directors: Rupert Barrington, Mary Crisp, Tim Lambert
Executive producer: Alex Graham

Printed and bound by
Butler & Tanner, Frome

HEADLINE BOOK PUBLISHING
A division of Hodder Headline
338 Euston Road
London NW1 3BH

www.headline.co.uk
www.hodderheadline.com

A CHILD'S WORLD

A unique insight into how children think

Dr Sarah Brewer
with Dr Alex Cutting

headline

Dedicated to Saxon, Roman and Sapphire

*Dr Sarah Brewer is the author of over
25 books, including:*

Planning a Baby?

The Complete Book of Men's Health

Super Baby

I Want To Have A Baby?

Increase Your Sex Drive

Pregnancy – The Natural Way

Detox Yourself

The Ultimate Stressbuster

Copyright © 2001 Dr Sarah Brewer

Photographs copyright © 2001 Stephen Lovell-Davis
except those on pages 29, 109, 113, 121, 127, 171, 197,
208, 213, 227, 228, 236 and 237 copyright © 2001
Isabel Hernandez
The right of Dr Sarah Brewer to be identified as the
Author of this Work has been asserted by her in
accordance with the Copyright, Designs and Patents
Act 1988.

First published in 2001
by HEADLINE BOOK PUBLISHING

First published in paperback in 2002
by HEADLINE BOOK PUBLISHING

10 9 8 7 6 5 4 3 2 1

ISBN 0 7472 51185

Text design by Isobel Gillan

A CHILD'S WORLD
A Wall to Wall production for Channel 4 and
The Learning Channel in association with
Granada International
Series producer: Louise Rota
Directors: Rupert Barrington, Mary Crisp, Tim Lambert
Executive producer: Alex Graham

Printed and bound by
Butler & Tanner, Frome

HEADLINE BOOK PUBLISHING
A division of Hodder Headline
338 Euston Road
London NW1 3BH

www.headline.co.uk
www.hodderheadline.com

contents

foreword by Dr Alex Cutting • 7

chapter one
the mind reader • 15

chapter two
the lying game • 56

chapter three
the engendered species • 93

chapter four
the thinker • 131

chapter five
life and times • 166

chapter six
state of independence • 209

acknowledgements • 250

index • 252

foreword

a *Child's World* offers a rare insight into the lives of children. Go to almost any general bookshop today, and you will find hundreds of books on the subject – from weighty text-books about child psychology to parenting manuals, from personal stories of childhood to detailed books devoted to particular aspects of development. Important though these are, *A Child's World* is distinctly different in several respects. Unlike most books about child development, it takes you right into the world as experienced by children, and imagines what it must be like seen through their eyes. It is also unusual in that it focuses on six particular areas of child development, all of which are essential components of our humanity as adults. By combining what years of research have taught us about child development with direct quotes from parents describing their own offspring's behaviour, *A Child's World* provides a unique perspective on how children think, concentrating primarily on what is arguably the most important decade of our lives – between two and twelve years of age.

This has been an exciting project in which to be involved. The original idea for *A Child's World* came from Wall to Wall Television. Following on from their Emmy Award-winning series examining infant development from a baby's point of view (*Baby It's You*), Wall to Wall wanted to take things further. What is the world like for children? How does their understanding of the world and the people in it develop? What happens between infancy and adulthood?

The changes that occur in children's cognition – that is, their ability to think, reason and solve problems – between two and twelve years old are amazing. The thinking of a toddler is impressive, but distinctly limited when compared to that of an adult; the thinking of a typical twelve year old, on the other hand, is on a par with that of many adults. More cognitive development occurs in these ten years than in any other decade you care to choose within the human life cycle. Similarly, children's social development undergoes a massive change in these ten years. In this remarkably short space of time, a child changes from being a toddler who can speak only a few words, is utterly dependent on adult carers, has no real friends and only a very limited ability to understand or even play with others, to become a fully-conversant adolescent, who can stand on her own two feet, maintain many diverse relationships, pick her own friends and interact with others in complex and subtle ways. Again, there is no other decade in the human life cycle in which so much change in social development takes place.

Following on from *Baby It's You*, Annette Karmiloff-Smith, a world-renowned expert in cognitive development, agreed to be the series consultant for *A Child's World*. As the team at Wall to Wall, notably series producer Louise Rota, assistant producer Rosy Day, and researcher Andy Brown, began to gather ideas for the series, they decided that they needed to draw on research in social as well as cognitive development – which is where I came in, as a developmental psychologist specialising in both these fields. Perhaps more importantly for *A Child's World*, I have a particular interest in the links between these two areas of development. Children's thinking does not take place in a vacuum – it is influenced by other people from day one. Equally, social progress cannot take place without the ability to think, reason and learn. As such, social and cognitive development go hand-in-hand, even though many text-books describe each domain as if they evolved quite independently.

So, following a suggestion from Annette Karmiloff-Smith, I became involved in the project. From my point of view, it all started when several members of the production team from Wall to Wall turned up in my office one afternoon (albeit with an invite!), and started asking me difficult questions. What exactly *is* the skill of mind reading? Why can't young children tell white lies? How do you know whether a child has any understanding of morality? When do children make real friends? What I had originally envisaged would be a short, one-off meeting turned out to be the beginning of a long and productive relationship.

As the series developed, six topics crystallised from a welter of early suggestions. Each of these makes up one programme in the series, and thus one chapter in this book. Louise and her team wanted to focus on some of the most essential aspects of child development in those crucial ten years, in order to present what is, in essence, a universal picture of child development, whatever gender, race, religion or culture we come

from. So, for example, we all possess an ability to understand other people and their behaviour. We all have the ability to lie. We understand what gender is and why it matters. We can think in diverse and complex ways. We know about the human life cycle. And we possess the potential to become independent, self-governing adults. Of course, there are other areas of child development that are essential, but the six we examine in *A Child's World* are key areas – those which are common to us all, and which underlie many other aspects of development.

Although the general pattern of achievements in each of these domains is universal, I should also emphasise the importance of individual differences. These occur in all aspects of human development, and they are an inherent part of our ability to survive, flourish and evolve further as a species. In *A Child's World*, ages are given at which particular developments typically occur, but these are simply averages. So by definition, half of us will reach a given milestone slightly before this age, while the other half of us will achieve it slightly later, both positions being completely normal. Similarly, the length of time any one child spends at one level of development can vary widely. It is the order of development that is most consistent across different individuals, rather than the amount of time taken for it to occur. Some children crawl for months before walking, for example, while others almost skip the crawling phase altogether – but none learn to walk before they are capable of crawling.

The choice of the six topics has been a brave one, in my opinion. The subjects are complex and not always fully understood even by academics and other experts in child development. University students struggle to understand the development of thought, and I have spent many a long tutorial session helping my students grasp the complexities of mind reading. Wall to Wall, however, were determined that these concepts could be presented and explained clearly through the medium of television and in the accompanying book – and I think they have succeeded.

The amount of research that lies behind the final series and this beautifully illustrated book is phenomenal. As the series producer, Louise

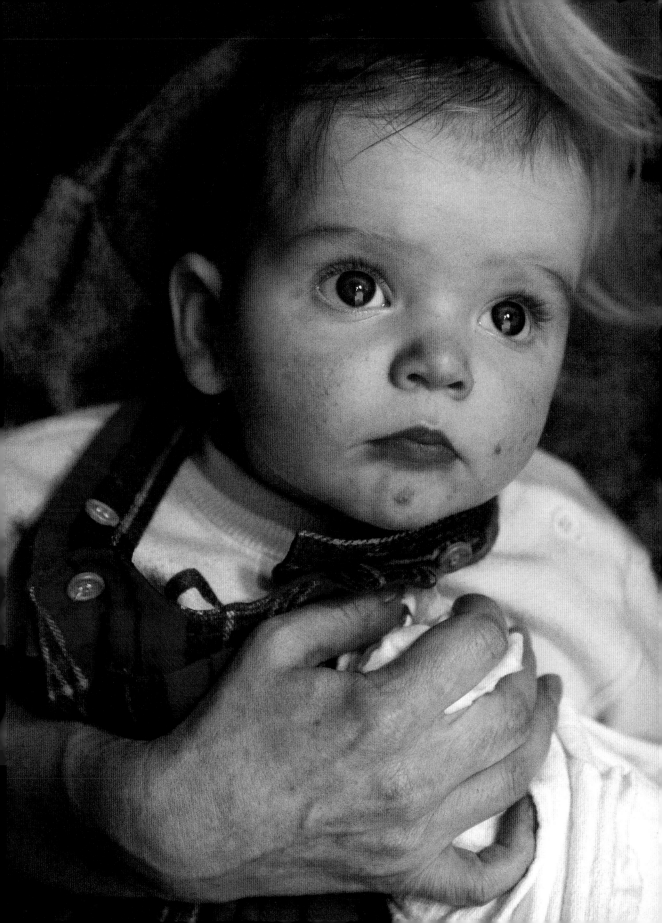

has been a powerful force; Rosy and Andy's enthusiasm and determination have been equally impressive, along with those of many others at Wall to Wall, simply too numerous to list here. I have lost count of the number of phone calls and e-mails I have had from Louise, Rosy and Andy, looking for clarification about one point, seeking more information about another, or just simply to ask yet more difficult questions! Rosy should get a special mention on this front, for such gems as, 'Where, *exactly*, is memory?' and 'Oh, can you just tell me how many thoughts people have every minute?' The answer to these questions is that nobody really knows – but they illustrate how much work lies behind *A Child's World*.

To produce a truly first-class series, the Wall to Wall team have had to teach themselves more child psychology than I would expect my students to cover in a year – and those at Wall to Wall have had to learn it in double-quick time. Louise, I suspect, could probably take over my teaching by now! The final series of six half-hour programmes is also the product of hours and hours of research and filming. The cliché about never working with children or animals must have sounded in the minds of more than one of the film crew as they patiently made their twenty-fifth attempt to capture on film a ten-second snippet of behaviour that the child demonstrated quite spontaneously before the filming started, probably several times!

In this book, we have been able to go even further, and the chapters provide more detail than can be squeezed into a time-limited television programme. The book has benefited enormously from the huge input of the questionnaire responses from parents and children. With the help of Annette, Wall to Wall sent out detailed questionnaires to nearly 200 parents, asking about their children's development and collecting quotes and anecdotes to illustrate the topics covered in *A Child's World*. The parents and children were volunteers who were recruited in London and Miami, Florida, who responded to advertisements placed in schools, nurseries, doctors' surgeries, newspapers, and even children's clothing shops! A few were veterans of *Baby It's You*, who had enjoyed taking part so much that they gave up their time for the follow-on series. Particularly important to the programme were three London schools who took part – Rhyll School in Kentish Town, St Michael's in Highgate, and the American School in London.

Finally, there is our valiant author, Dr Sarah Brewer, who sifted through the reams of quotes and comments from parents, not to mention the collected (and sometimes confused!) notes of several researchers at Wall to Wall, and the constantly changing scripts and programme plans, to put together this lovely book. An experienced author specialising in health- and child-related subjects, Sarah had to write this in record time. In my role as an additional consultant, I have had the pleasure of editing and developing the chapters in order to present the clearest insight possible. This book is not aimed simply at students or academics, but at anyone with an interest in child development. The only qualification you will need to enjoy this book is to have been a child yourself!

ALEXANDRA L. CUTTING, Reading, April 2001

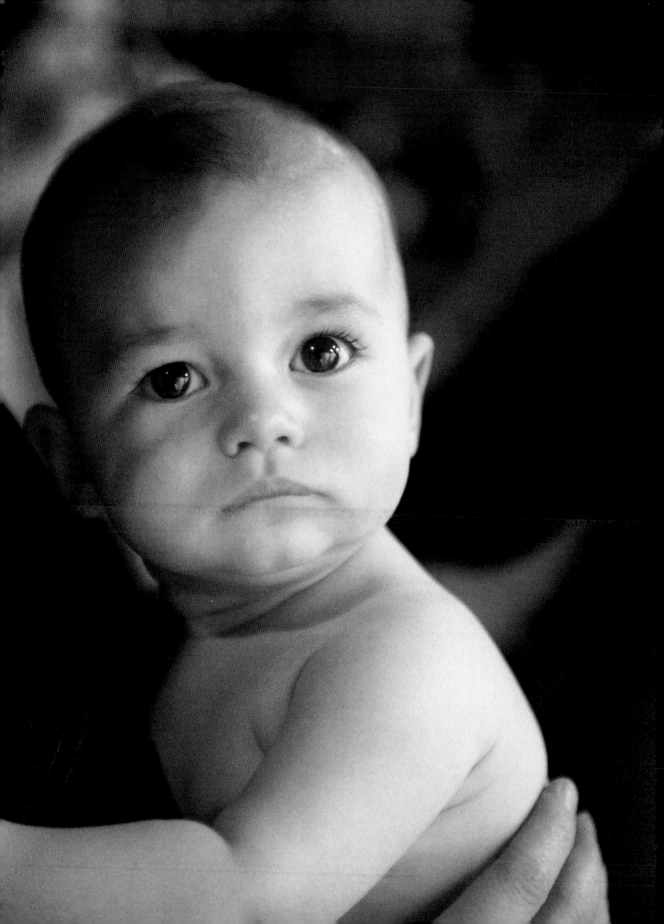

chapter one

the mind reader

do you realise that you are a mind reader? In fact, the vast majority of people are. Every day, we have to use mind-reading skills, working out what people are thinking, imagining how other people are feeling in any particular situation, or trying to understand what someone means or intends.

We live in a world full of individuals who think, feel and act according to their own view of what is happening around them. In order to survive in this complex social environment, and to interact with other people in an acceptable way, we have to learn to understand the world from other people's perspectives. It is only by standing in their shoes like this that we can hope to understand the intentions behind their actions, and judge how to respond appropriately.

Mind reading is a uniquely human skill and, although it may sound complex or even mystical, it is something we do subconsciously every waking hour of every day. We use mind reading when trying to understand what an eighteen month old with limited language actually wants. It is mind-reading skills that tell us almost 'instinctively' when a friend who says she is 'OK' really isn't. Our ability to mind read helps us to work out when someone is joking or teasing, and then enables us to tease back!

Put simply, mind reading is the ability to understand people's behaviour in terms of what they are thinking or feeling. That does not mean we actually know exactly what a person is thinking when they behave in a particular way, but we do know that they must be thinking something and we can usually come up with a sensible guess about what

Though vital to our species, mind reading is not a skill we are born with that is. Our understanding of people as thinking beings is so automatic that if we see someone do something odd we often say something like 'What is he thinking of?' or 'Has she lost her mind?'.

In many jobs, the ability to understand another person's thoughts and feelings is essential. Imagine a car salesman trying to sell the same car to three different customers. The salesman knows that different people want different things from a car. His job is to work out what each customer wants, and then to emphasise that feature of the car and try to persuade the customer that this car is just what he or she wants.

So the salesman will probably chat with each customer at first, being very attentive as he looks for clues about that person's particular likes and dislikes, thoughts and feelings. As well as trying to come across as trustworthy and likeable, a good salesman quickly works out what his customer is thinking and then tries to turn that to his advantage. Perhaps he will emphasise the safety features of the car to a family with children, the speed and style of the car to a young bachelor, or the economy and reliability to an elderly couple. In each case, the salesman must use his mind-reading skills and if he does it really well, chances are the customer will not even notice!

We also rely on mind reading when communicating with others; communication is really about understanding what other people are thinking. We need to know what our friends, relatives, partner, colleagues and boss are thinking whenever they communicate with us, whether they use voice, postal mail, e-mail, fax or even carrier pigeon. A modern city literally hums with the noise of people communicating verbally and electronically. We are a social species, which makes mind reading absolutely vital. Not being able to mind read would be a significant problem. Indeed, people with autism lack this skill and their ability to understand others and interact with them is seriously impaired; a person with autism might accurately be described as living 'in a world of his own'. Yet surprisingly, given its importance, mind reading is not a skill we are born with. It is something we have to learn during the early stages of our development as human beings.

Me, myself and I

A newborn baby is isolated from the world in the sense that he or she has a limited ability to communicate with others. This is where we all begin, unaware that we even have a mind, let alone that it is surrounded by millions of others. A newborn baby seems to have no concept of individuality – his own or anyone else's. It is as if the baby thinks that everyone is a part of him and he is a part of everyone else.

A baby doesn't even know that he _has_ a mind

The first stage in a baby's development as a social animal is to recognise that he or she is an individual, separate from the rest of humankind. Once he knows this he can begin to understand that we are all individuals, and that even though we interact we are all independent. A baby does not start with a completely blank sheet on which he has to build the mental skills necessary to survive in an adult world, however. He actually starts a step or two up the mind-reading ladder, because he is born with several abilities that help him learn about the social world and

Babies have no concept of where they end and others begin

his place in it. He is already able to identify with his own species, for example: if a human baby hears the young of another species crying – such as a dog yelping or a kitten mewing – he will not respond. If he hears the cry of another human baby, however, he will respond as if he, too, is upset and will also cry or at least look unhappy until he is comforted or distracted. This innate crying-together reflex, sometimes called 'contagious crying', is one of the reasons why a nursery area in a maternity ward can be an incredibly noisy place!

Babies also learn to discriminate between adult and young faces very early, during just the first few months of life. Interestingly, they also recognise and focus more on other babies than on older children and adults. Psychologists don't know why this is, but possibly in the drive to be part of their own species, a baby is programmed to recognise those who are most similar to him or herself before recognising that he or she is a separate individual.

However, babies soon start to realise that they are separate individuals. The initial sparks of a sense of self are usually evident by the age of six months when infants already have a wealth of experience interacting with people, toys and the world around them. This phenomenon is especially noticeable to the parents of twins:

> When Roman and Sapphire were first born we had to rush to pick a baby up if he or she cried, before the other one started. They easily set each other off. It's not so bad now they're six months old. If one cries the other tends to just study him or her with a quizzical look on their face, unless it's feeding time and they both feel hungry.

The growing sense of self can be explored using mirrors. Before the age of three months a child will show little interest in his or her own image, or that of anyone else. From about four months, the baby will start to smile at and reach out towards a reflection of a toy or another person and try to touch it, as he clearly does not realise that it is only an image he can see. By the age of ten months, however, if he sees an object being hidden behind him while looking at his reflection, he understands

Eighteen-month-old Rosie is starting to realise that
the face looking back at her is her own

enough to start reaching behind his back to find the toy. He does not
seem to recognise himself, however, as he will not try to touch a smudge
on his own nose or forehead even if he sees it in the mirror.

It is not until a baby is around eighteen months old that she appears
to recognise her own image. This is perfectly illustrated when a child
who has accidentally got a splodge of paint on her face looks in a
mirror. A child who does not recognise herself will reach out towards
the mirror, not realising that the paint is on her own face. By about
eighteen months of age, however, she will reach up and touch her own
face and explore the paint spot she has just seen in the mirror. This

shows that she clearly recognises her own reflection. By the age of two, self recognition is well established. If a two year old looks in a mirror at her own reflection and someone asks 'Who's that?' she will quickly answer with her own name. At this age, a child can pick herself out in a photograph and starts to use words like 'I' and 'me'. She now has an indisputable sense of self.

A sense of self and emotion

Self awareness is an integral part of children's social and emotional lives. By the age of one year, babies experience and express at least six important human emotions in response to events in their immediate world. These are: joy (for example, when playing peek-a-boo), surprise (at being startled), sadness (such as when left alone), anger (when dropping their favourite toy and not being able to reach it), fear (when confronted by a stranger or loud noise) and disgust (when experiencing a new taste they dislike). Although these emotions are all direct responses to events around them, they contribute towards a child's developing personality and growing sense of self.

As that sense of self develops, infants start to experience and express several new, more complex emotions, such as embarrassment, pride, shame, guilt and envy. These complex emotions all rely upon the development of self awareness and the sense of having one's own will – each reflects an enhancement or injury to the sense of self. Once a child starts experiencing these more complex emotions, such as envy or pride, he must already be able to think about himself in relation to other people. These emotions are therefore described as 'self-conscious' emotions.

Embarrassment and envy, which just require a basic sense of self, appear from eighteen to twenty-four months. Pride, shame and guilt begin to appear around two-and-a-half years of age; to experience these emotions, a child must have not only a sense of self, but also a standard

Holly, eighteen months, is beginning to gain a sense of her own identity

of behaviour against which to compare him or herself. Such emotions are therefore sometimes described as 'self-consciousness evaluative' emotions as they involve the child comparing himself with others and recognising when he is 'better' or 'worse'. This in turn either boosts or dents his sense of self accordingly.

Self-conscious emotions are mainly learned from adults' instruction – different behaviour is seen as being shameful in different cultures, for example, and children need to be taught what is appropriate in their own society. A child will quickly work out what behaviour earns praise and what leads to a 'telling off'. Adult teaching sets the ground rules, so that a child knows the standards that are expected and learns how to act appropriately as an individual in a social world.

Working out where I end and you begin . . .

Once a child has a sense of self, he can begin to work out the difference between 'self' and 'other'. Learning to interact with others and noticing differences between people provides the foundations for the mind-reading skills that have yet to develop.

At two years of age, a child has begun to develop a clear sense of self, but is still unaware that other people have 'selves' too. A child's words and actions can appear to be very selfish at this age, but psychologists argue that this is not really the case. One child may take another's favourite toy, refuse to give it back and carry on playing with the toy quite happily, even when the other child is obviously upset. Although this is easily interpreted as selfishness, a child of this age is, in fact, only capable of thinking about what he or she wants and cannot see that someone else might not want the same thing. He wanted to play with the toy and was unaware the other child thought differently. Possessiveness about toys and shouts of 'Mine!' are thus very typical of two year olds, as these examples illustrate:

Maxim, two, is very proprietorial about his toys and will shout at, or tell off, any child who takes something of his.

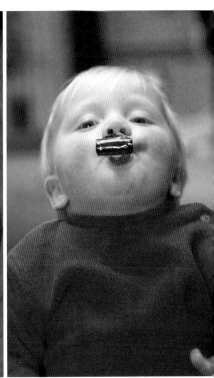

Around the age of two children appear possessive,
thinking everything belongs to them

Jashan, two, has started to enjoy the company of other children greatly, and looks forward to seeing them. He wants to play and can be quite charming and kind, but with those he is closer to, he can also be pretty aggressive and intolerant – he hits Aaron and can have trouble sharing toys with him.

However, this is not really selfishness. Selfishness means caring too much for your own needs and not enough for the needs of others. A two year old is not yet aware that others even have needs, so does not realise that snatching toys upsets other children. Early conflicts over toys really reflect an increasing sense of self and the child's efforts to work out how far that self extends. When the wronged child snatches back, it provides an early lesson in the difference between 'me' and 'you'!

Self-conscious emotions and early conflict are important steps forward in the mind-reading game as they indicate that a child has a clear sense of self and is starting to discover that the emotions others are experiencing are not the same as his or her own. Realising that other people have different feelings also helps children develop another important social skill – that of empathy. For example:

> If Maxim, two, hurts any of us he will immediately say, 'Sorry, Mummy' (or whomever he has hurt) over and over again.

> If Rebekah, three, knocks into me or hurts me in some way she now says, 'I'm very sorry Mummy', and seems concerned, which is a new phenomenon.

When confronted with someone who is obviously distressed, a child will also start trying to give comfort – always assuming he or she didn't cause the upset in the first place (in which case comfort is less likely to be offered!). The following are typical:

> If his older brothers, Theo or Fabian, are hurt or upset, Maxim, two, will go to them and try to kiss and cuddle them better. I also remember an occasion when I dropped and broke a plate that I really liked. Fabian was only three years old but he understood how upset I was and opened up his arms to give me a hug.

> I hurt my knee recently and Jashan, who is almost three, very lovingly rubbed and kissed it better. Sometimes I think he must understand that other people's thoughts and feelings are different from his own, but I'm sure he doesn't always.

> When Dad cut his finger, Amy, three, was concerned and got him a plaster. When I was ill, she lay a blanket on the floor.

At this age, children's attempts to help are often endearing but inappropriate as the blanket on the floor, quoted above, suggests. For example, when Natasha, two, noticed that Daddy seemed upset while arguing with a plumber on the telephone, she went up and offered him her favourite dolly to cuddle by way of comfort. Although Natasha was aware of her father's feelings and wanted to comfort him, she offered what she, herself, would find most comforting. At two, she still only sees the world from her own point of view and assumes that what makes her feel better will work for her daddy, too. Even though a two year old now recognises her own individuality, she still assumes everyone else sees the world exactly as she does.

Taking another perspective

As adults, we know that everyone sees the world from a different perspective, both literally and in terms of their opinions or points of view. We use our mind-reading skills to understand these different perspectives. Young children, however, do not realise that different perspectives even exist. Instead, they assume that their own perspective is all that there is and that it is shared by everyone.

You can see whether or not a child still thinks everyone else sees the world from his own perspective by observing how he reacts to common everyday questions. For example, if you ask a child looking at a photograph (you cannot see the picture) to show you what he is looking at, he will usually hold up the photo towards him so that only he can see the picture and you cannot. He assumes that you can see what he is seeing.

This behaviour is perhaps most obvious when talking to a child on the telephone. When Carmen, two, was asked 'What did you get for your birthday?' she just offered up the present to the receiver without saying anything by way of explanation. Because she assumes that everyone else sees the world from her own perspective, she expects the person on the other end of the phone to be able to see the toy she is proudly displaying. Similarly, when asked whether or not she liked the present, she only nodded her head vigorously at the phone, without saying 'Yes'. This shows she does not realise that the person on the other end of the line cannot see her response. The following diary quotation is also typical of this behaviour:

> Tarran is two, and when his grandma rings up she asks him what he's doing. We've got a cordless phone so he takes it over to where he's been playing with his construction toys and holds the receiver right over the tractor. We often shout 'He's showing you the tractor', or whatever, so she can respond to him.

Another everyday example of this phenomenon occurs when Daddy comes home from work and asks his two-year-old toddler to fetch Daddy's slippers for him. The child will happily toddle off and get them, but when he brings them back will place the slippers on the floor facing towards himself, as if he were going to put them on, instead of facing them towards his father.

This self-oriented perspective applies not just to the child's visual perception of the world, but to her thoughts and emotions as well. Even though she has a sense of self, and recognises her own individuality, she still assumes that everyone else thinks and feels just as she does. It's not that a child doesn't see the need to focus outside herself, it's just that, at this age, she is not aware of other perspectives and thus is unable to imagine them.

Interacting with others

Having a very personal view of the world means that friendships between toddlers are often deceptive. Children may appear to show great interest in each other and seem to be friends, so that when you watch them from a distance they look as if they are talking and playing together. When you come close enough to pick out their individual voices, however, you soon realise that they are not talking with each other, but at each other.

Maxim, two, does talk to his brothers, but it's not really a conversation, more of Maxim making a statement and his brothers repeating it back to him.

Aaron, two, recently went through a stage of repeating the name of whatever friend the older children had to play. When they replied, he was just quiet, i.e.
Aaron: 'Milo.'
Milo: 'Yes.'
Aaron: (silence)

Ten seconds later, Aaron: 'Milo.'

Milo: 'Yes, what?'

Aaron: (silence)

And so on for hours. Luckily he seems to have grown out of this one.

I suspect Jashan, who is almost three, just talks at his friends. But he can't stop!

Ellie and Bobby, both two, rarely interact with each other even though they seem to be 'friends'

Two year olds tend to play alongside rather than
with one another

Similarly, two year olds are not yet able to play games together, because they are still unaware that others have minds different from their own, so they cannot yet share their thoughts and emotions. To play together, children need to be able to take account of what each other does or does not know. Unable to manage this, two year olds play alongside each other rather than truly playing together. Psychologists call this 'parallel play' and the following quotations are typical:

Maxim, two, is still at the stage where he just plays alongside children of his own age. He is very good at playing on his own. He will push cars around or line them up.

Oliver, two, and James, two, love to play with the train set. But they don't play together. Usually they both take a train and play on separate parts of the track!

Rianna, two, likes to play with her older sisters. Usually they get involved in role play like mummies and daddies. Rianna gets very involved in her role play but her conversation is more practical and her sisters get frustrated when she doesn't manage to follow the idea of the game or really join in.

As a child gets older his or her verbal skills improve. However, while he remains oblivious to any view of the world other than his own, he will have more satisfying interactions with adults than with other children: adults are better than children at 'filling in the gaps' in a child's conversation, working out what the child is trying to say and making sure the child (as listener) understands.

Young children tend to communicate by making statements and, when talking together, they leave lots of gaps in the conversation as they still cannot judge what the listener already knows or does not know. As a result, they miss out important bits of information and may not make sense to anyone else. If a class of nursery school children come back from a trip to the zoo, for instance, one child may say to another, 'Snowy was big and white and ate lots of fish,' and the reply may appear nonsensical, such as, 'It was blue,' because the other child is picturing the bucket the bear was feeding from at the time. A conversation like this does not last long!

In contrast, adults are better at gathering information they lack by asking appropriate questions. When a mother hears her excited child say 'Snowy was big and white and ate lots of fish', she will use her mind-reading skills to identify what information she still needs in order to understand what her child is trying to tell her. She will probe further, ask the right questions or make educated guesses to fill in the conversation's blanks and keep the interaction going. The two can then have a meaningful conversation about the polar bear at the zoo, and the mother can pass on information to expand her child's knowledge of the animal world. This is something that other children of the same age cannot do. Children therefore tend to improve their conversation and develop their social skills more easily by talking with parents and other adults than by talking with youngsters of their own age. The following quotations are typical of children at this stage:

> Lana, three, plays well with older children and likes to play mother to smaller ones, but has difficulty playing well with her peers. She thoroughly enjoys the company of familiar adults.

> The children don't really talk about anything to each other but sometimes Rebekah, three, asks questions that she's heard me ask, like 'What did you do today at school, Josh?' She doesn't really wait for an answer. She says things like 'I want to talk' and 'Let me talk now' but then can't think of what to say. She wants us to stop talking so she can get in on the conversation but doesn't know yet how to join in . . . She is jealous of my giving attention to other adults and puts her hands over my mouth or tries to pull me away from them. She often says 'Shut up, Mummy, shut up.'

Let's pretend!

As children learn about their world and the people in it, they become increasingly aware of other people as individuals. Between three and four years of age, they begin to understand that other people have their own minds and thus their own points of view. The ability to pretend plays a particularly important role in this development. Because pretence takes place 'all in the mind', it is a wonderful introduction into how the mind works.

At first pretence is very simple, occurring when a child playing with one object pretends he is actually playing with something else. For example, when three-year-old Jashan's sisters are practising on their musical instruments, he will take a cardboard tube and ruler and pretend

At age three, Ewan's verbal skills are improving, but he will still find it hard to have a conversation with his older brother Alex

that they are a violin and bow. This type of pretend play is sometimes seen as early as eighteen months and is usually well developed by the age of three. Being able to pretend in this way means that the child can set aside what he knows about an object (for example, that it is a ruler with which you measure things) and substitute this knowledge with his own interpretation (that it is a 'bow' with which he can play a 'violin').

In this kind of play the child doesn't actually believe that a transformation has taken place but is able to pretend, and that's the critical thing – she can now hold two different ways of seeing the same thing in her head at the same time. This helps her start to understand that there is more than one way of seeing the world and that her point of view is not the only one. In a way, she has learned to manipulate reality as she is not just seeing the world as it is, but is also imposing her own imagination upon it.

By three years of age, most children are accomplished pretenders. They now know that reality can be manipulated in their own mind. The next step is to understand that other people have minds, which means that they can have their own points of view, and can also manipulate the world. At this stage, a child becomes able metaphorically to step into someone else's shoes. This first happens when he or she pretends to be someone else such as his or her mummy or daddy. At this stage, however, when children dress up and play cowboys and Indians, or doctors and nurses, their play is simplistic and they are simply mimicking the words and physical actions they have heard and seen others speak or do. The child cannot yet imagine what it is actually like to be a mummy or daddy, or a doctor or nurse, and does not as yet understand the different points of view that accompany these roles. They copy without really understanding what it means to be the person they are pretending to be – in effect, they are adopting the person's actions, but not their thoughts.

Nevertheless, by pretending to be someone else the child is, for the first time, becoming aware of how things may look from someone else's perspective. He or she is teetering on the brink of becoming a mind reader. Make-believe play now makes up a significant part of a child's play:

The current role-play favourites for Abigail, three, are mummies and babies, Cinderella and her prince, and the Big Bad Wolf.

Jashan, three, plays Batman and also, when the girls are playing vets, he'll be the dog or even the baby!

Lana, three, likes to pretend to be a monster or fierce animal and 'eating people up'. She doesn't like it too much if you do the same to her.

Alice, three, is often acting fantasy roles playing out marriage dramas, otherwise she just chats away non-stop about everything. Marriage and romance feature large in her life.

Interestingly, psychologists have found that children often use a different type of language when playing in their imaginary world compared to what they use in the real world. For example, French children were found to favour the past tense for pretend play even before they used this in their everyday life. Perhaps this helps them to separate the real from the non-real in their minds before the difference becomes second nature.

Once a child can 'step into' someone else's mind, she may even invent an imaginary friend, which may help her to practise her mind-reading skills and learn more about social interactions. This is especially likely with children who don't feel ready to interact with real friends, or don't have the opportunity to do so. Imaginary friends are therefore more common among first children who do not have other close siblings or peers to play with (although this is by no means the rule), and they can appear over quite a wide age range as the following quotations show:

Theo had an imaginary friend when he was two. Her name was Nina.

Joshua, three, has an imaginary friend whom he pretends is someone from *Chitty Chitty Bang Bang*.

Twins Francesca and Sicily, four, have lots of imaginary friends – animals mainly. Sicily has an imaginary cat family in Ireland.

Joanna, five, has a teddy bear, Bertie, who is an imaginary friend. She and Bertie have long conversations and sometimes he even has supper with us.

As children become more and more adept at pretence, they become able to share their pretend world, taking part in what psychologists call 'joint pretence'. They can get involved in role-play games together and pretend together that a cardboard box is a house, or a boat, or a spaceship. Now they are able to understand each other's pretence and not just their own.

Similarly, two children playing together become able to accept that an item they are both playing with represents something completely different to each of them. For example, if they are playing with some small boxes, one child may pretend that a box is a car and say 'Look how fast my car goes!' while the other might reply 'It's a good car. I'm making it a tiger – look how fast my tiger can run!' They are happy to accept each other's version of what the box might be and that the two of them are looking at things in different ways. This shows that they have taken another crucial step along the road to mind reading: they fully realise that their minds are separate and can hold different points of view. To reach this understanding a child has, in a sense, stepped not just into the shoes of the other, but actually into his or her mind and looked at the world through his or her eyes.

The mind reader

The key skill in mind reading is to be able to work out the thoughts, feelings and beliefs behind someone else's actions. A child's grasp of this concept is accompanied by a rapid expansion of short-term memory and thinking power, allowing him to build up memories that help him work out links between what people do and why they do it.

Before a child can manage to make these links, the world can sometimes seem a confusing and frustrating place. During a trip to the cinema, for example, three-year-old Ewan was allowed to select an

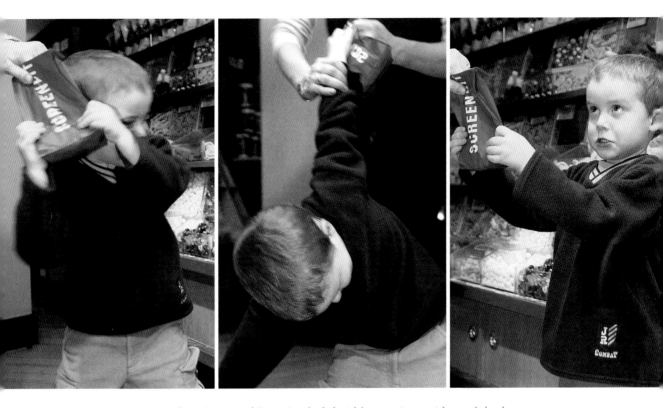

It hasn't crossed Ewan's mind that his sweets must be weighed
and paid for before he can have them

assortment of sweets from a pick and mix counter in the foyer. When the
bag was full, his mother tried to take the sweets from him, intending to
get them weighed before giving them straight back. As Ewan was unable
to read her intentions, he refused to give up the sweets and a scuffle
ensued. In Ewan's mind his mother was confiscating the sweets and he
might never have got them back. Once he has gained mind-reading skills,
however, and his memory allows him to recall that the last time his sweets
were taken they were given straight back, Ewan will start to appreciate
the intention behind his mother's actions and 'read' her mind in a similar
situation. Other people's actions will then become meaningful, so that
rather than just observing what someone is doing, he will have moved
on to what comes next and maybe even why they are doing it.

Like with most stages in a child's development it is rarely possible to identify a specific point at which he or she actually learns this mind-reading skill, which is known to psychologists as having a 'theory of mind'. Having a theory of mind means that a child has worked out (i.e., has come up with the theory) that people have minds, and he understands that it is the thoughts and ideas in those minds which govern people's behaviour. Parents often notice when their child is beginning to understand the concept of other people having distinct thoughts and feelings:

Alice, three, is beginning to realise that other people have different thoughts and feelings and plays on this, saying 'What do you think, Mum, do you think this or that' etc., as a kind of teasing game.

Rebekah, three, is beginning to notice that people have different thoughts and feelings. She will note 'Daddy's angry, why are you shouting at Mummy? What's she done?' Or if I tell her off, she says 'I'm going to tell Daddy, he's going to shout at you.'

Although the onset of mind-reading skills is gradual, and there is no single 'Eureka' moment when a child suddenly understands what is going on, it is surprisingly easy to discover whether or not a child can read minds, using a simple test known as a 'false belief test'. A child who passes the test has become a mind reader.

Show a child a container that typically contains one kind of thing with which they are familiar, such as a piggy bank with money in it. Rattle the piggy bank and ask the child what he or she thinks is inside. He or she should say 'Money' in this case. You then empty the piggy bank while the child is watching and put different items inside such as marbles. All you then have to do is ask the child what she thinks another person (who is outside the room and so has not seen the piggy bank emptied and the marbles inserted) will think is inside the piggy bank now.

Ewan, three, and Abigail, four, are being tested to see if they have acquired mind-reading skills yet

If the child has attained mind-reading skills, then she will know the other person will think the piggy bank contains money and will often laugh in delight as she says this, because she knows the other person is bound to give a wrong answer when asked what is in the piggy bank! But if the child has not yet achieved mind-reading skills, then she will still assume that everyone else – including the person outside the room – sees the world exactly as she sees it and thus knows what she knows. She will therefore say that the other person thinks the piggy bank contains marbles.

Trimaine, three, fails the 'false belief test', showing he has not yet acquired a theory of mind

All children are different, and the age at which they learn to mind read can vary quite widely. Typically, children gain mind-reading skills between three and four years of age. By four, most are able to understand the links between what people think and how they behave. Interestingly, children with brothers or sisters to watch and learn from tend to acquire mind-reading skills slightly more quickly than first-born children. This is possibly because they have more experience of situations in which the links between thoughts and behaviour are especially relevant, such as teasing, tricking each other, joking and talking about feelings. Parents do not always tell their children how they feel, but a slighted older brother or sister rarely has any qualms about doing so!

Once a child has learned to mind read, parents often become aware of a shift in their child's thought processes and realise that their child now has a better understanding of other people. For example:

Reece, four, does sometimes realise that different people have different feelings from his own, like when someone is upset.

I think Akira, four, understands that people have different personalities, thoughts and needs (but he doesn't always accept it).

Ellie, five, understands that people have different feelings and understands about traits such as shyness or different abilities according to different ages.

Mind reading allows both children and adults to appreciate each other's differing opinions, likes and dislikes, and allows children to start understanding how their actions affect others. It also allows them to start being helpful and considerate as they can now mentally step into other people's shoes and understand how they are likely to feel, or what they might think, in a variety of situations, as these following examples illustrate:

Leon, four, offered to make tea for Daddy in bed. He went into the kitchen, returned with a child's plastic cup and said, 'I'm sorry, Daddy – it's not real – I'm not big enough.'

Suzanna, four, often says, 'I like your hair/trousers/ top.' She will also
get out my breakfast, and tidies up her room 'as a surprise'.

Khalil, seven, knows other people have different opinions – not
something he always likes or with which he concurs. He may say, 'It's
not your cup of tea, Mummy, but I like it.'

Today Kishori, five, successfully avoided upsetting her brother by
NOT telling him we had had lunch in McDonald's.

The children in the above examples have all thought about the world from
someone else's perspective. Leon realises that his Daddy will not think
there is real tea in the cup, even if he, Leon, pretends there is; Suzanna
knows that her mother enjoys certain activities that she might not like
herself; Khalil is well aware that he and his mother have different tastes.
Kishori has taken things a step further, and not only knows that telling
her brother about McDonald's will upset him, but is also able to keep her
treat a secret. As Kishori demonstrates, children's ability to feel empathy
for others is also well established by four to five years of age, as the
following quotations from parents of four year olds confirm:

Suzanna, four, is very sensitive and aware. She can tell when you are
'sad' and often plays tricks or gives you cuddles to make things better.

Georgie, four, definitely realises people have thoughts and feelings
different from her own. She will ask 'Are you happy, Mummy?' or 'You
look sad – has a sad thing happened?'

The ability to read the thoughts behind someone's deeds is a complex
skill, yet it has developed well enough by the age of four for a child to
distinguish between things done on purpose and things done by accident.
This ability helps us to respond appropriately in a variety of situations,
and if someone does something wrong it helps us know whether to
respond with anger (because it was deliberate) or with sympathy and
understanding (because it was a genuine mistake).

When Saxon, four, breaks something by mistake he gets quite upset and keeps saying 'Sorry, it was an accident.' If he has broken something he shouldn't have been playing with, however, he becomes even more upset as he knows he has done wrong. He is wily enough to say something disarming like 'Please don't be cross with me.'

Jake, five, got very angry when his older brother broke a toy car on purpose. Another car got broken last week when it got caught behind the toy box, but he didn't mind that so much, I think because it was an accident.

Being able to understand another's intentions is a vital social skill because what people intend or mean is not always obvious from the actions they take or the words they say. Once a child understands this, she can judge how to respond, taking the situation into account. For example:

Kishori, five, is an exceptionally good girl and will always do what she perceives to be right. She shares well and plays beautifully with other like-minded children. When confronted by less perfect behaviour, however, she can get quite upset and tends to seek solutions from an adult or, if it suits her, allows the other child to 'get away with it' so that the play can continue.

Children's conversational skills are also improving now, although they still tend to talk at each other, and often over each other, as the following quotations show:

Twins Francesca and Sicily, four, still mainly talk at other children rather than listening to what they have to say.

Tavey, four, chatters away about things he has done but the conversations aren't always very linked with those of his friends. There's not much listening – more talking at them. He likes chatting to adults and likes to be the centre of attention. He is quite a charmer.

I take Rebecca, four, and two of her friends to school in the car on a regular basis. She tries to listen but does interrupt to put across her own views and opinions. The noise level in the car is very loud as at times all three of them are talking about different things to one another and they just get louder and louder.

A whole new world

Attaining mind-reading skills is perhaps the single greatest step in a child's psychological development. At first it is rather hit and miss, and a lot of learning and honing of skills is needed before the child can fully become part of the complex adult world. Once this step is made, however, a whole new world starts to open up. Without mind-reading skills, there could be no conversation, no relationships and none of the symbolism that we enjoy in books, films and art. Irony, sarcasm and jokes would prove impossible. Of course a child who has just begun to mind read does not suddenly become able to understand and take part in the world just like an adult, but her world will become hugely enriched in many different ways.

Play, especially pretend play, becomes more complex and probably much more exciting once a child can step into someone else's mind and really understand their perspective. Where a child may previously have just pretended that a cup was a racing car, he will now pretend he's the racing car driver and start to act and think as he imagines a world champion racer needs to act and think. He can now develop wonderfully involved and complicated scenarios and even share them with family and friends, like these children:

Rebecca, four, role plays mummies and daddies, doctor and patient, hairdresser and client, and shopkeeper and customer. She also talks to her toys, especially her favourite teddy, Snowy. She recently held a birthday party for him in her room, just her and Snowy. She made a card for him and wrapped up some of her toys for him as presents.

> We have hundreds of little characters at home we call 'shelf people' and these shelf people all have their own personalities and complex relationships with each other. Many of them have to come on holiday with us – it would be hard to imagine Emily, five, and Alice, three, going a day without their shelf people.

Instead of just simply stepping into the shoes of another character and mimicking their actions, children now begin to create emotions and motivations for that character and to interpret the intentions and motivations of the characters their friends have created. A favourite game of seven year olds Holly and Anmika, for example, is to work through a complex role-play scenario revolving around 'Vets in Practice'. The girls are the vets and they make Theo, five, and Kishori, five, be the animals that they wrap in bandages, give medicine to and operate on. The following extract gives another typical example:

> Emily, five, plays games that are 100 per cent fantasy and always has; she acts like a theatre director with her peers, saying 'You be this' and 'I'll be that', and 'We'll be doing this', etc. She role plays more often than she lives her 'real' life.

The more children indulge in this form of mind-reading play, the more they hone a number of newly acquired social skills such as negotiating for roles and taking turns. At around six or seven years, they develop the ability to hold the thoughts of two or more other people in their mind at the same time, and understand that they can be in touch with minds that are in touch with other minds to form a large mind-reading network. Once this ability is in place, children understand complex ideas such as 'I know that he knows that I know', and they are able to take part in fantasy games involving several others, as suggested below:

> The children all love dressing up as princesses and pirates, kings and queens. One particular role model of Holly's, seven, is the queen from *Alice in Wonderland*. They play lots of imaginary games: mothers and fathers; hairdressers; hospitals; teachers is a particularly popular one.

Our children (ages two, four, six and eight) play complex teachers and
pupils games. They will set out paper and pens for imaginary pupils
whom they will give names to. When playing recently Bradley (four) told
Mark ('Child's World' researcher) not to talk and that he, Bradley, was
not allowed to talk because the teachers (other children) were very strict!

Another area in which the ability to read minds has particularly profound
impact on children's lives is that of friendship. As a child's mind-reading
skills become better and better, friendship takes on a whole new meaning.
Children do form friendships before they can read minds, but these early
friendships are often based on shared activities (such as going to playgroup
together) or are the result of a friendship between their parents. Before
they can read minds, young children tend to regard a friend as being
'someone to play with' or share toys with. As children grow older and start
to mind read, however, they start to understand friendship as being a
relationship based on mutual liking and intimacy:

Katie, five, says she likes her best friend Amber because 'She's good
and kind and we take turns to play with our Barbies. She doesn't
snatch and she likes me. And she told me a secret.'

Children can now share thoughts and feelings, and are more interested in
what other children think and say than in the toys they possess, although
materialism still plays an important part in bolstering self esteem:

Ellie, five, and her friends talk about each other's possessions –
stories, videos, characters they are familiar with such as Cinderella,
Sleeping Beauty, Tarzan – sometimes competitively.

Anmika, seven, talks about material possessions she has or hasn't got,
comparing each other's toys, clothes or music.

Self esteem is now increasingly important because, once you have mind-
reading skills, you need to feel good about yourself before you can
imagine that others will feel good about you, too. As well as depending

on a sense of self worth, close friendships help to foster self esteem in a self-perpetuating cycle. Children understand very quickly that, although their parents love them unconditionally, friends tend to love conditionally. So the very fact that a friend wants to share her thoughts and feelings tells a child that she is a worthwhile person. When a child acts positively towards someone else, she not only observes the pleasure she has the power to bring, but, as a mind reader, she can also imagine how good the other person feels.

Mind-reading skills also help children develop more selective friendships, as they are now able to identify like-minded souls who have a similar view of the world, similar abilities and who can share similar interests and activities. Children are now able to judge who they want to be friends with and are also able to adapt their behaviour to fit in with different groups. For example:

> With unfamiliar children Holly, seven, is quite cautious. If she doesn't know someone she may watch for a while before joining in.

> Khalil, seven, will vary his behaviour depending on the children he is with. He tends to be more boisterous and bossy with similar children, and quieter and more reflective with quieter children. On the whole he prefers more active children.

> Jack, five, is somewhat of a shy child. If he enters a group of children he scopes out the scene carefully, finds the kids who are playing with something he would enjoy playing with and slowly integrates himself into their group.

In addition, children now have a sense of time and future, which means that they can understand the value of investing effort in a continuing friendship rather than abandoning it and repeatedly starting all over again with new friendships. It becomes easier to understand that a continuing friend is someone who can be relied on when you are in trouble, who can lend you things and share jokes and secrets, as well as admiring you and supporting your sense of self.

Around half of children aged around five or six have one main friend with whom they spend over a third of their time. When fall-outs do occur, however, mind-reading skills help children make up again. They can now think about why something happened from another person's point of view, and they can also negotiate and work out how they can influence that person to think differently. As a result, friendships can be patched up and maintained over a long period of time. Some childhood friendships are maintained right through to adulthood.

Having several friendships also helps children learn about differences between relationships. They will discover that they can be dominant over one child but will find themselves being more submissive with another. Children are very sensitive to their status in their peer group from this age onwards, and actively use their mind-reading skills as they work out their own place in the 'pecking order' of their peers. The following quotations describe typical behaviour in five and six year olds:

Eleanor, five, is beginning to be horrid to children she has to play with whom she doesn't like.

Emily, five, seems always to have been aware that other people have different feelings; her problem has been how to manipulate people so that they think and feel in the way she wants them to!

Amanda, six, is nice to the children she likes, but can be a bit horrible to the ones she doesn't like.

Perhaps most importantly of all, mind-reading skills help a child imagine what it is like to be left alone without friends, and therefore help to promote generous and altruistic behaviour. For example:

Elizabeth, six, is a soft touch, regularly complaining to me because she has given away her last sweet.

Rory, seven, makes decorative boxes full of old toys to give as Christmas presents to a charity – he's getting a broader social conscience now.

By the age of five, children understand why it's good to share

Becky, nine, is very concerned about kids being left out. For example, she invited a girl to come trick-or-treating for Hallowe'en with us because she's new here and Becky was upset that she didn't have anyone to go with.

Being able to appreciate other points of view allows a child to think about other people's likes and dislikes. A child may, for example, spend a lot of time in a toyshop selecting just the right birthday present for a friend, based not on what she herself would like to have as a gift, but on what she thinks her friend would like to receive, drawn from her knowledge of her friend's likes and dislikes. This shows that the child knows and cares about the feelings of other people. Children can now behave in ways that are essentially unselfish, for instance:

At school they made collages of a Christmas stocking and went through an Argos catalogue choosing and cutting out what presents they wanted, and stuck them in their stocking. Theo, five, chose a Barbie and a Tweenie, not for himself as everyone else had, but saying he wanted to give them to Holly, seven, and Aaron, two.

Kishori, five, is very much aware of other people's thoughts and feelings. Whenever she has something for herself, she always thinks of her brother and sister. Recently, when hiring her a cello, she insisted on buying her sister a badge from the music shop so that her sister would not feel left out.

Emily, five, often draws lovely cards with nice messages on if Rory or Alice hurt themselves, for example, 'Dear Rory, I am so sorry you hurt your leg', etc. 'Dear Great Granny Figgis, I am so sorry you are so old' was intended to be considerate!

When sweets were brought in for the whole class to celebrate Khalil's birthday, one child was allergic to sugar. Khalil insisted that he should buy something for her so she didn't feel left out – so he gave her a small perfumed, fruit-shaped soap.

Kishori, age five, can think about what sort of toy her friend would enjoy playing with

Children at this age are also much more sensitive to others' distress than they were as three or four year olds, and may even put the welfare of another child before their own feelings:

> Khalil, seven, seems quite sensitive to others' distress – even strangers who look upset. He might say 'I think that man/lady looks upset, Mummy.' He once comforted a distressed classmate by putting his arm round him and saying, 'It's OK. Just calm down and we'll go and see Miss Ross.'

> Corey, seven, will give in to other children if they are upset, if they are a close friend. When a little girl spilt juice all over his Pokemon cards he was devastated, but when she continued crying he went up to her and told her that it didn't matter. This is a big deal as Pokemon cards are like gold to him.

Related to their developing ability to understand others' feelings and provide appropriate comfort, children who can mind read often start to develop a strong sense of fair play, as they are now able to recognise when someone else is (at least in their opinion!) being treated wrongly, as illustrated in the following quotations:

> Anmika, seven, often defends her siblings if they are being told off. She is also quick to defend her father if ever I sound critical of him: 'He can't do that Mummy, 'cos he's at work.'

> Nicola, six, complains that others (mainly children) are not always as kind and thoughtful as she would be to them and can't accept the difference.

As their mind-reading skills develop, children also become as good as adults at asking questions to fill in the gaps in their knowledge if the information they are presented with is unclear.

> Rory, seven, is starting to interact with adults very well, asking questions, offering information about himself, and is learning not to interrupt.

Around the same time – by the age of seven or eight – children also realise that, just as they can read and influence other people's minds, so other people can read and influence theirs. They begin to understand the notion of trust: children of this age will say that they trust their friends, which is something a five year old would not understand. Of course children also learn that not everyone can be trusted – it is much more difficult to fool an eight year old than a five year old!

As children learn to trust appropriately, they will also start to judge another's intentions based on prior knowledge of that person's behaviour. This allows them to give the benefit of doubt to friends who seem to be acting badly, while remaining suitably suspicious of what may be deceitful, rude or unfriendly behaviour in strangers.

With maturity and the development of higher levels of reasoning, children become able to maintain friendships even after a serious difference of opinions. Because they value a friendship, they may use their mind-reading skills in a positive way to withdraw before a situation escalates enough to get out of hand. If a fight does break out, they may stay nearby afterwards and try to minimise the importance of a conflict once the dust has settled. Reflecting this, over three-quarters of nine-year-old children in one study were found to have the same best friend at the beginning and end of a school year compared with just over half of those aged six. The following quotations sum this up beautifully:

Danielle, eight, plays with most children but tends to stay away from rough boys and from girls who tell her what to do all the time. A couple of girls in her school have tried to separate her and her best friend, without success so far.

Mary, nine, has a small number of good friends to whom she remains loyal for a long time. For example, she became close to a girl in her class while we were living in Moscow 1994–1997 and still asks to see her.

From late childhood onwards, friendships are increasingly based on trust, loyalty, shared secrets and mutual understanding, rather than focusing on shared activities. Children also find the role with which they are most comfortable – whether leader, follower or a bit of both:

> Taliesin, nine, is mainly a leader with his peer group, but there are occasions when he is happy to follow.

The darker side?

Although they are essential in human society, mind-reading skills do not come with a set of instructions on how best to use them, and like most other things in life, there is potential to use them for bad as well as for good. Before they had mind-reading skills, children only knew how to hurt each other physically by hitting or biting. Learning how to mind read, however, gives children more than just new ways of understanding the world; now they also have a whole new set of weapons.

Now, if they wish, children can use their ability to read minds to manipulate the thoughts and emotions of others in negative ways as well as in positive ways. They can deliberately make others unhappy by manipulating their thoughts, or go out of their way to please people so they are accepted into their group. Just like adults, all children try this out as they continue to explore different forms of behaviour. For example:

> Anmika, seven, is generally warm and considerate. She is particularly kind to younger children although she has a tendency to be extremely bossy. She can be mean to her siblings, however, taking advantage of their age to tease them or manipulate them. With older girls, she can get very excited and desperate to please.

> Rory, seven, is quite assertive in a clever way; he has learned how being polite can get what he wants.

Some children develop bullying behaviour, however, and it is often assumed that bullies have poor social and mind-reading skills and fail to understand the effect that their behaviour has on their victims. New research suggests the opposite can sometimes be true, however, and that some 'talented' bullies have a very well-developed theory of mind. They know exactly how to manipulate a situation and other people to hurt their feelings. They also know how to do this in a way that minimises the chance of getting caught.

Using mind-reading skills to manipulate or hurt is by no means the exclusive domain of children of course. By the time we have reached adulthood, we are masters of manipulation and can, if we wish, use our mind-reading skills to exploit or bully others and to apply powerful forms of emotional blackmail. More positively, we can also use these skills in subtle and socially positive ways to boost our own and others' self esteem, to motivate and to help everyone achieve their full potential.

The mind-reading skills we acquire in childhood, and continue to practise throughout our lives, allow everyone to function in a complex, social world. Role play, which was used to help us interpret others' intentions and emotions in childhood, takes on a hugely important part in adult life. Every adult – whether they are a parent, vet, teacher, salesman, criminal or judge – plays many social roles and puts on a different front depending on the impression they wish to give or the behaviour they know is expected of them. Their tone, manner, actions – even the words they choose – will change according to the circumstances in which they find themselves. We all role play all our lives, even when we are unaware that we're doing it. Society and even civilisation depend on it.

chapter two

the lying game

the vast majority of us are accomplished mind readers. We are also accomplished liars. Almost as soon as we learn to read minds, we learn how to deceive them. As adults we are skilled at lying – we can hide our feelings or act as if we feel quite differently than we do, we can lie about our opinions and pretend that we know things that we do not. Ask an adult whether he lies and he will probably do just that: 'I don't really tell lies' (is this one?!).

In fact, lying is an essential social skill and most of us are likely to lie several times a day, if not more. Sometimes we tell serious lies, intending to deceive someone for our own benefit, but mostly we tell fibs (harmless or trivial lies) and white lies (lies intended to prevent someone else's feelings getting hurt). These small distortions of the truth actually help to keep life ticking over smoothly.

If you find this shocking, just imagine what life would be like if we always told the truth. For example, let's visit a dinner party at which the host, Guy, has suddenly been deprived of the ability to lie. The doorbell rings and Guy answers it to find Sarah and Bill on the doorstep holding up a bottle of wine. Guy looks surprised, but instead of pretending to be pleased to see them, says 'Hello. That's funny, I thought we'd agreed not to invite you. There's nowhere else you could go, is there?' Sarah and Bill laugh awkwardly but don't answer, so Guy says 'No? Well never mind, it just means less food for everyone else . . .'

Children become more adept at lying as they grow older

Later, when eating his starter (which is clearly very small and cut in half) Guy takes a mouthful, dislikes it and, instead of pretending it tastes good, suddenly spits it out, saying, 'Ugh, yuk. It tastes like filth.' When Jane asks Sarah, 'How's that lovely little boy of yours?', instead of smiling politely, Guy interjects, 'You mean the Pig?' and when Jane says, shocked, 'Guy, no!' he replies blithely, 'Oh, you meant the other one – the Reptile.'

During the after-dinner chit-chat, when things have calmed down a little, Guy carries on with the social tact of a raging bull. Remember, he is not doing anything wrong, he is merely telling the truth because he has lost the ability to lie. But clearly, there are many occasions when the truth simply will not do.

Telling lies is not always for our own benefit. Adults have to tell lies in many social situations, often to avoid hurting people's feelings or simply to fit in with socially accepted norms. Indeed, our lying skills are often used for good reasons and show that we are sensitive to other people's needs and feelings; our mind-reading skills are sufficiently advanced that we are aware of what people want to hear and what they do not.

While it is easy to condemn children for telling untruths, it is actually an important skill, although one they must learn to use wisely. Children must not only learn how to differentiate the truth from a lie, they must also understand when telling the truth is a bad thing and a lie is more appropriate. Lying is such an essential adult skill that, quite simply, if children did not learn how to do it properly they would soon become social outcasts.

Children's ability to play 'the lying game' is thus intricately linked to their understanding of morality and socially acceptable behaviour. At the same time as coming to grips with the etiquette of lying, children also have to learn to distinguish right from wrong. They must learn self control and to treat other human beings (and their belongings) with respect. Morality does not seem to be inborn, however; it varies between different cultures. Children learn what is right, wrong and socially acceptable or unacceptable from those around them, and adult teaching is an important part of the process.

The early days: learning how to behave

Although a long way from being able to lie, a baby takes his very first steps in the lying game when he is very young. Parents unconsciously 'shape' their infant's behaviour almost from day one. Any signs of 'positive' behaviour, such as an early smile, are responded to enthusiastically with attention and returned smiles. A howling baby certainly gets a response too, but that response is rarely as enthusiastic! These differences in response are subtle and largely unconscious, but they are already teaching the baby about what is socially acceptable behaviour and what is not.

For his own part, a baby will also notice very early in life that there is a link between his own behaviour and that of the people around him. Soon after birth, he will start to appreciate that he can affect someone else's actions and trigger particular responses. For example, he will learn to cry when he

Babies learn through people's responses to their behaviour

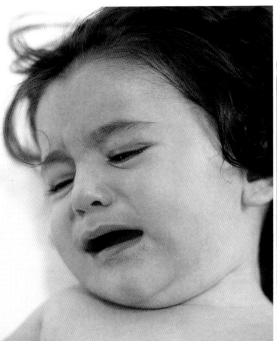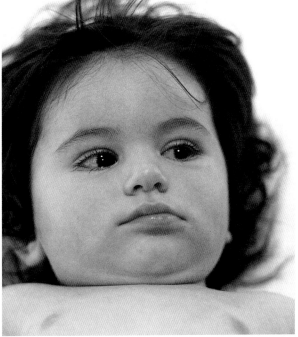

wants to be fed, changed or comforted, or to smile when he wants attention or a sociable interaction. As a baby gains more experience, he learns to communicate in many different ways in order to get what he wants:

> At the age of six months, Roman has learnt that whenever he wants attention, he just has to make a repetitive noise, 'Uh, uh, uh, uh' over and over – increasingly loudly – until someone picks him up. Then it's smiles all round.

Roman already knows how to manipulate his care-givers in several different ways, although at this stage there is obviously no deception involved in his actions.

Once a child understands that there is a link between his behaviour and the response he gets from others, he can learn to get what he wants by behaving in certain ways and saying certain things. By the time he is a toddler, adults can begin to teach him the rules of acceptable social interaction more directly. For instance, a mother will teach her child to say 'please' and 'thank you', and the child will learn that he is rewarded with what he wants only if he uses these special words.

Although the child initially has little understanding of what these all-important words actually mean, he learns quickly that he must use them to get the desired response. Taking another step towards playing the lying game, he will soon learn how to use these new words for his own benefit. On a cold winter's day, two-year-old Louie was out for a walk with his dad when he spotted an ice-cream van. He asked if he could have an ice-cream, but his father refused the request. Louie asked again using the word 'please', but the answer was still 'no'. Determined to get his ice-cream, Louie pleaded, 'Please, please, please, please, please, please, PLEASE can I have one?' Worn down (but impressed!) by Louie's persistence and attempts to play by the rules, his father eventually gave in. Although there is no deceit involved, Louie is learning how to manipulate others to do his bidding, using a skill he has been taught by an adult.

Louie, two, has learned that saying the magic word will get him what he wants

It is the responses of those around them that teach children about the desirability of their behaviour. Children are not born knowing what is right or wrong – as any parent of a toddler will tell you! However, they soon start to realise that 'good' behaviour is rewarded with praise or treats, while 'bad' behaviour is frowned upon or leads to a telling off:

Holly, eighteen months, still doesn't realise the difference between right and wrong until you tell her. For example, she'll tip a drink over the carpet and smile at you, expecting a smile back. When she doesn't get one back, but a cross face instead, then I think she realises she's done something naughty.

Freddie, eighteen months, is learning what is right and wrong from his mother

Joss, eighteen months, doesn't really know right from wrong – he just knows there are things he shouldn't do, like putting socks in the loo.

Aaron, two, knows treats are for good children and if I say he's naughty he says, 'No, I'm a good boy.'

As a result of feedback from others, especially adults, children start to understand the difference between good and bad behaviour, and their reactions will show that they know when they have been naughty:

Tré, twenty-two months, knows the difference between right and wrong because if he's done something wrong and knows it, he hides under the bed.

Jessica knows when she does something wrong but at two she still does it. She will sit and colour on the table or door. When she is discovered she runs, knowing she has done wrong.

Getting attention and avoiding trouble

As children become more aware of what is acceptable behaviour and what is not, they gradually discover how to adapt their behaviour to get what they want. Until they are aware of the existence of other minds, this type of manipulation is not true deception on the part of the toddler, but it is probably where 'true' deception begins. Children aged two to three years notice the effects that their words and behaviour have and are remarkably good at using what they notice to their own advantage. Once a child notices that behaving in a particular way gets him what he wants, he will often use that behaviour freely, even if it is based on something which is not true:

Oliver, two, wakes up early and shouts to us to come and get him up. Last week we didn't come at once (hoping that he'd go back to sleep!). After several bellows, he yelled, 'Daddy, I'm pooing!', which got an instant response. Now he yells that every morning, though it's not true.

Similarly, a good example of what is easily misinterpreted as deceptive behaviour comes from Aoífe, aged two-and-a-half, who regularly uses the same trick to gain attention. When her sister and friend are doing their homework in the kitchen, Aoífe runs in and says that she has hurt her hand. Her sister strokes it and says, 'Poor Aoífe', before sending her to the fridge for ice to make it better. Aoífe runs off, happy for the time being, but five minutes later she's back. Unaware how transparent her ploy is, she continues to repeat the scenario until her sister, fed up, sends her packing. Although Aoífe is technically telling a lie, she does not recognise it as such – all she wants is the attention that she knows her words will bring.

Neither Aoífe nor Oliver is being deliberately deceptive. Both are simply repeating an action that received attention last time round and assuming that it will work again. Even so, both children have now learned, by themselves, to suggest something – a dirty nappy or a hurt finger – which is simply not true. Similar behaviour is often seen when a young child wants to avoid something, such as a pit stop when playing or getting ready for bed:

> Maxim, two, will often tell me he hasn't done a poo when he has because he hates being changed. Or else he'll tell me that Daddy or Raquel (our baby sitter) has changed him, even if he hasn't seen them for ages.

> Jashan, two, only tells fibs about very obvious things, for example, 'I'm not tired' or 'I don't need a wee'.

At this stage, children are also beginning to juggle with ideas of what is right and what is wrong, and they often start experimenting with shifting the blame onto someone else. At the age of two, this type of behaviour is more an effort to avoid trouble than a conscious attempt to deceive a

Aoífe's trick doesn't fool anyone after she's repeated it three times, but it shows she is starting to learn the rules of the lying game

parent into thinking that someone else is responsible for the behaviour in question. For example: Natasha, two, tore off a strip of wallpaper in the dining room. Her mother asked her if she did it. Natasha said, 'No. Bradley did it' (her brother, aged four). Her mum replied, 'Bradley did not do it,' to which Natasha said, 'No, Danielle did it' (her sister, aged eight). 'Danielle didn't do it,' said Mum, so Natasha tried again: 'No, Amanda did it' (her sister, aged six). When her mother said, 'Amanda did not do it, you did,' Natasha said, 'No' and ran under the table to hide.

Louie, two, knows when he's done wrong because he starts laughing and runs away. Whenever he is being naughty and is about to get in trouble, he says his little brother Rio, who's only one, did it.

Abigail, three, sometimes blames her younger brother for things even though he's only five months old – usually about all the toys being everywhere.

Another excellent example occurred when three-year-old Ewan was painting a picture in the kitchen while his mother decorated a chocolate cake with sweets. The doorbell rang and, leaving Ewan with strict instructions not to touch the cake, his mother went to answer it. Alone with the cake, Ewan eyed it up before glancing towards the door. After tentatively poking his finger through the icing he covered up the hole he'd made with a sweet. Then, he took a sweet, sucked it and put it back. Eventually, throwing caution to the winds he got stuck in. Hearing his mother coming, however, he quickly stopped what he was doing.

'I told you not to touch it!' she exclaimed.

'I didn't!' said Ewan (his hand covered in chocolate).

'Then who did?' asked Mum.

'Alex,' replied Ewan, blaming his older brother who was at school at the time.

Ewan's deception is utterly transparent

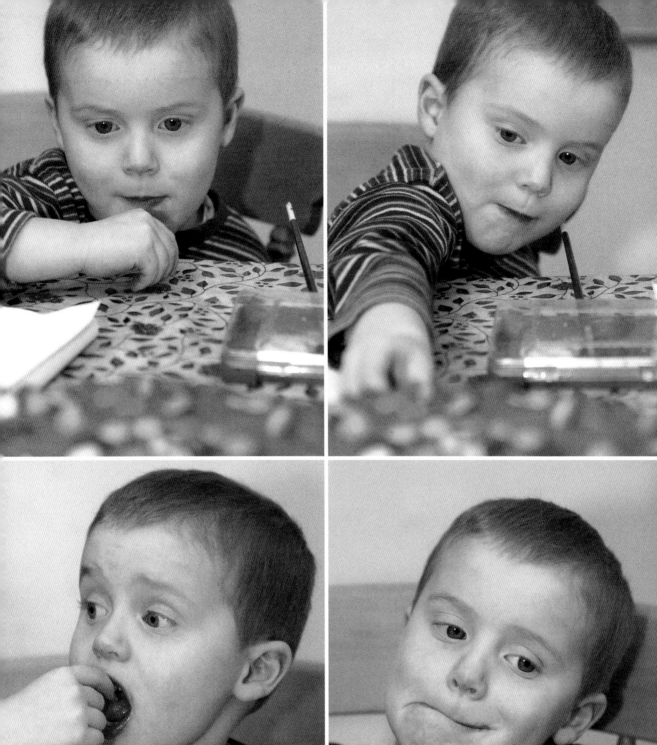

The very impossibility of the 'lies' described above shows that the children do not really understand deception – Natasha just repeats her strategy of blaming someone else every time her mother thwarts her, until she has run out of people to blame; Louie and Abigail lay the blame on a sibling who is far too young to have committed the misdemeanour in question; Ewan blames a sibling who is not even at home and he seems oblivious to the fact that his mother can see his chocolate-covered hand!

Ironically, children at this age will also often tell the truth in situations where an older child might lie, or at least avoid being completely honest. Not understanding deception means that young children will sometimes tell very obvious lies, but it also means that sometimes they are scrupulously honest and do not realise that a lie might be to their benefit! For example:

> When Thomas came into the room crying, we asked Sam, two, who was holding a toy hammer, if he had hit Thomas. 'Yes,' he said, not batting an eyelid!

> James, two, showed me a lovely picture the other day. I said, 'That's great, did you draw that, James? It's lovely', all ready to praise him, but before I got any further he said, 'No, Alex [a friend] did it.'

Learning the rules

Young toddlers often appear quite selfish in their interactions with others. For example, they may take toys from others, not react to the upset it causes and then throw tantrums when made to give the toys back. As explained in Chapter 1, this type of behaviour reflects the fact that young children see the world only from their own point of view and assume everyone else does too. Because of this single-minded view of life, young children see what is right or wrong for them as being right or wrong for everyone else too. Their moral reasoning is limited; it is essentially a case of 'I want it, so I should have it', and they will justify their 'naughty' behaviour (if at all!) with their own needs and desires.

Maxim, two, is too young to know that he shouldn't take things that don't belong to him. He will take whatever he feels like taking but is very possessive of his own things.

Oliver, two, gets angry when I return toys that he has taken from other children. He'll shout, 'No, Mummy! I want it, I want it', and it's hard work distracting him from whatever it is.

Helena, two, works on the principle that whatever is hers is hers, and whatever is yours is hers also. She is very aware of what belongs to whom and woe betide anyone who touches her toys without her express permission.

These two year olds have not yet learned that other people have different feelings, or that society expects them to behave according to certain rules. They will learn from experience and adult teaching, however, and will soon begin to grasp the idea of responsibility. By three years of age, most children have started to form their own ideas about what constitutes good or bad behaviour.

Rebekah, three, tells me if her brother or sister have done something wrong, for example, 'Mum, Josh hit me', 'Zoe's playing with the television', 'Josh is naughty. Is he naughty, Mum?' She also gets worried if she thinks I'm angry at her for making a mess and she quickly says sorry and tries to clean up.

Joshua, three, went outside and did a wee on the floor. I told him off and he went straight upstairs – he knew it was wrong.

Trimane, three, can tell the difference between right and wrong because if he has done something right he looks for praise and if he has done something wrong he says he didn't do it, or changes what happened.

Once they start to grasp the rules about what is acceptable behaviour and what is not, children will often test them, to work out exactly where the boundaries are and ensure that the rules are consistent. At this stage in their development, children may therefore seem to misbehave deliberately to test their parents' rules:

> Amy, three, knows it's wrong to kick, but will still do it and say her foot just patted you.

> Rebekah, three, now quickly says sorry and tries to make amends when she is naughty, for example, hitting her sister. Sometimes she doesn't though and stubbornly refuses to say sorry.

As children start learning about morals and forming basic rules in their own minds about the difference between right and wrong, they start to appreciate that adults around them sometimes do or say things that don't fit in with these rules. When spotting a parent do something wrong, they may become quite upset or angry. For example:

> If I knock something over or do anything he perceives as wrong, e.g. coughing without covering my mouth, or not finishing my dinner, Jashan, two, tells me I'm a 'naughty Mummy'.

> Rosa, three, is starting to realise the difference between right and wrong more and more and will accuse others (people she knows, people on TV) of being naughty or 'not nice' when they are unkind or aggressive, etc.

> Trimane, three, will tell me off for swearing, and if I promise to do or give him something and don't, he gets very upset.

> Both Euan, three, and Finlay, six, can recognise right and wrong and tell us (sometimes they get very angry) if we are rude, stressed or impatient with them.

Fact or fiction?

Children between the ages of three and four are on the verge of becoming mind readers. They are accomplished pretenders by now and, as we saw in Chapter 1, pretend play is an important part of learning how to read other people's minds and imagine what they are thinking. There is also rapid growth in children's memory and attention span at this age, which enables them to create increasingly elaborate, imaginative stories – an important part of learning to lie, because effective lies often require subtle skills of imagination. The fine line between fantasy and out-and-out lie eludes a child at this stage, however; they will often 'stretch the truth' and play with different 'versions' of reality:

> Lana, three, has a vivid imagination. She told her keyworker that she has a pet dog and cat. She also swiped her sister's lolly when she wasn't looking and gave it to her dad, saying that she had bought it from the shop especially for him.

> Rosa, three, embellishes stories that have an element of truth, for example, when she clashes with her father, she accuses him of shouting at her for no reason.

> Emily, five, often pretends she has an entirely different name and identity – even in nursery she would only answer to the name Belle, and all her paintings came home with the name Belle on them.

These children are not lying; they are not deliberately sowing a false thought in another person's mind. It is fantasising, and although a child may mislead someone during this process, that was not the main intention. A child at this age may expect an adult to believe her story though. This is partly because the child does not have enough experience of the world to recognise the boundaries of possibility and absurdity, and partly because the child is still unable to appreciate that other people do not see the world as she does.

Fantasies, tall stories, white lies and genuine, intended deceptions are all based on untruthful statements, however, so how does a child learn to tell the difference between what is a good, embellished tale and what is an actual lie? Generally a tall story is designed to entertain and make people laugh, while a lie is designed to bring the teller some benefit that they would not otherwise receive.

Although this distinction may be obvious to an adult, it is a difficult concept for a child to grasp. Children hear their parents and friends exaggerating the truth all the time when recounting daily events and may notice that, like Chinese whispers, these embellishments can grow with every telling. Children also hear their parents tell small fibs and white lies. They spend much of their time living in fantasy land, hearing stories of princes, beasts and magic spells. They are surrounded by cultural legends, myths, novels, films, TV soaps and boastful advertisements – so how do children learn the difference between truth, exaggeration, acceptable white lies and lies that are bad? The only way is to tell a few stories/lies and stand back to await the reaction. If children are rewarded with praise or laughter, they learn that it was a good tall story or white lie; if they receive a telling off or a moral lecture, they learn that the lie was bad.

Parents and other care-givers shape a child's understanding of truth and lies through their own approval and disapproval. When assessing the 'badness' of a lie, most of us quickly weigh up several things in our minds and identify a good lie as one that is harmlessly amusing, makes us laugh, spares another's feelings or boosts someone's self esteem. In contrast, a bad lie is one that is harmful, manipulative, covers up some wrong doing, brings an unacceptable advantage or is deliberately designed to manipulate someone else's beliefs in a bad way, such as to their disadvantage. This is both a difficult line for an adult to draw and a difficult one for a child to learn.

Lana, three, blamed Carmen, nineteen months, for scribbling on the floor, but with encouragement admitted it was her.

Children start to understand the moral 'rules' of lying in a fairly 'all or none' way. Lies are initially understood as being 'bad', so that the concept of a trivial fib or white lie does not make sense. Many children will become quite upset at this stage if they recognise that an adult is telling a white lie; this seems to go against the rules they are starting to understand about what is good and what is bad, and – quite understandably – they become confused.

> Changing plans at the last minute and trying to explain with a white lie can really upset Rosa, three.

> Georgie, four, picks us up on white lies immediately and will cry if, for example, we've said the video shop is closed and she spots that in fact it's open.

> If Abigail, three, hears me tell a white lie, she is confused and she will ask question after question until you admit the fib, for example, we can't go to the park because it's closed – why? etc., etc.

Liar liar

To truly be able to lie, and to recognise that someone else is lying, children need to understand that other people have different thoughts that can be manipulated. They therefore cannot tell real lies, designed to deceive others, until their mind-reading skills are in place.

We can discover whether or not a child understands basic deception using a simple hiding game. Take a button or penny and tell the child that you're going to play a hiding game. Put both hands behind your back, hide the button in one, then put both fists out in front of you. Ask the child to guess which hand the button is in. Do this three times so that the child gets the idea, then say it's her turn to trick you. Children who do not yet understand how to deceive may not bother to put their hands behind their back to hide the button, or may give the game away by showing the button in an upturned palm, or perhaps sandwiching the button in between both hands. They may even tell you which hand it is in! For example, when asked to hide a coin so that an onlooker had to guess which hand it was in, Ewan, three, put his hands together and then opened them so that the coin was visible. Until a child is able to conceal the whereabouts of the button, he cannot begin to conceal the truth.

Once a child has learned how to deceive, he still needs to hone his skills – the ability to lie convincingly does not emerge overnight. As such, children's first real lies are often not very convincing to adults. A child who understands what lying is, but who is not very good at it, may hide the button described above perfectly well, but still gives the game away by trying to ensure, with a very obvious lie, that you choose the wrong hand.

The simple hiding game reveals whether children understand deception yet

A typical example of this is for a child to hold his hands out, saying loudly, while giggling, 'It's in this hand, it is. It really, really is!' By lying so badly, he gives away that the coin is actually hidden in the other hand. These quotations describe similar examples:

> When Ewan, three, and Alex, five, were hiding a monkey toy, they stood in front of where it was hidden and told us not to look there.

> When I brought Granny a birthday present recently, I told Saxon, four, that we mustn't let Granny see it as we brought it into the house. As we went through the kitchen with the present in a large carrier bag, Saxon said to Granny in a loud voice, 'This present is for no one, Granny. It isn't for you.'

Lana, age three, is still too young to deceive others properly; she can't help giving the game away

When children first start telling proper lies and deliberately trying to sow false thoughts in someone else's mind, they do not understand that lying is not just about the words used. They don't realise that their false words must be backed up with an appropriately straight facial expression and normal body language or the lie will be transparent. Inexperienced liars often give themselves away, for example by going red in the cheeks or through a mannerism:

> When Alex, five, tells a lie he always puts his tongue in his cheek, so his mum always recognises he is lying.

> Rory, seven, had a favourite story when he was younger in which a baddie smuggled jewels into Heathrow airport and the customs men could tell he was lying about what was in his case because he didn't look them in the eye – he looked sideways. Rory has always remembered this story and, try as he might, he cannot tell a lie without looking sideways.

A lot of children adopt these mannerisms when they first start telling proper lies. It shows that they have enough understanding of the moral difference between right and wrong to know they are trying to be naughty, but not enough experience or understanding to hide their naughtiness effectively. Another common giveaway is seen when a child opens her eyes wide when telling a lie, as she tries to convince her listener that she is innocently telling the truth. Similarly, children who do not yet have the skills needed to back up their lies and the false impression that they are trying to give will often contradict themselves, giving the game away:

> Georgie, four, occasionally tells a fib – but obviously knows she shouldn't and qualifies it by saying 'Only joking'.

Young children learn fast, however, and feedback from others helps them to work out what is effective when lying and what is not. It does not take long for a child to realise that his actions must back up his words if he is going to successfully make someone believe something that is not true. At first, a child may match his behaviour to his words fairly simply, such as by hiding the evidence when claiming to have done something that he has not:

> Akira, four, sometimes throws food in the bin and says he has eaten it.

> When Leon, four, was offered Smarties if he ate his porridge, he hid it in the fridge saying, 'I've eaten it, now can I have my Smarties?'

Children at this stage may also try a variety of different lies and actions, such as stealing. Trial and error and adult teaching then help them to work out which behaviour is 'good' or socially acceptable and which behaviour is 'bad' or anti-social enough not to be tolerated, whatever the circumstances.

> Our son, five, does take things that don't belong to him if they appeal. I was amazed last week because he had taken a shoe horn from our guest's shoe and was happily taking it to school before I noticed. I think he knows they don't belong to him but thinks that it doesn't matter if he plays with them for a while.

When learning to lie, children also need to understand the difference between a deliberate act (for example, a lie) and a mistake (for example, a misapprehension). If someone tells them that they cannot play on the swing because it is broken, for example, they need to judge whether that person is deliberately trying to mislead them or really believes that the swing is broken. If they are found out telling a lie, they also need to judge whether to come clean and admit they were lying, or whether to blame their falsehood on a mistake. Children soon learn that a mistake or accident is not intended and is thus less serious, in moral terms, than a deliberate deception. As they become mind readers they may even start to try to use this to their advantage:

> If Saxon, four, does something wrong he usually says it was a mistake or an accident. If he perceives a wrong against himself, however, he will proclaim very loudly that it was done on purpose.

A moral code

At the age of four, children are still learning the rules about acceptable behaviour, even though they are now able to lie. They have yet to understand the subtle differences between lies, fibs and white lies, and are still learning that most lying is regarded as unacceptable. Conflicts and the responses of others now play an increasingly important role in moulding children's moral judgements about what is right and what is wrong.

> Tara, four, will sometimes do something beyond the family boundaries and then give a challenging look, often with one hand on her hip.

If one child hits another child, for example, things usually end in tears or anger and a scolding from an adult. This gives the child direct feedback about how bad his moral violation was. He also sees how upset or angry his friends are as a result of his behaviour.

> Tavey, four, knows it is wrong to fight, etc., but it doesn't stop him doing it. It is always a huge battle to get him to say 'sorry' if he has hurt one of his brothers.

Children's early moral sensibility is self oriented. Toddlers, being unaware that other people have thoughts and feelings of their own, do not consider much beyond their own needs and desires – they simply are not aware that anything other than their own point of view exists. Moral sensibility in preschoolers begins to reflect their developing understanding of rules about behaviour. Children at this age tend to focus on the outcome of their behaviour and regard certain actions such as hitting as 'wrong' because it gets them into trouble. As they learn from others, generally adults, what is right and wrong, their moral understanding also begins to reflect their society's moral conventions: they are beginning to understand the concept of responsibility for their own actions and the moral standards that society expects of them. These children, for example, know clearly that certain behaviour is unacceptable (even though they will still do it!):

Rebecca, four, can differentiate between right and wrong. I have heard her tell her friends not to hit each other. She knows not to lie and her school teachers say she has a strong sense of justice.

Jack, five, will hit his sister and I will ask him if that was right to do. He will tell me 'no'. He finds it quite disturbing when a friend of his hits him or yells at him because he knows that is the wrong thing to do.

By four or five, children understand that other people have thoughts and feelings of their own, which allows the development of a more interpersonal moral sensibility. Although children at this stage of development still act in their own interests, when asked if their behaviour was good or bad, they will now usually say that what they did was wrong if it upset someone.

Ellie, five, knows when she has said something spiteful to someone in the family as it upsets her when she says it and afterwards she attempts to make up for it by being extra sweet, compliant, etc. She recently told me she hated me but was contrite enough later on to tell me she loved me, which she doesn't often say.

Between the ages of four and six, moral issues cannot yet be seen in shades of grey, such that doing wrong may be acceptable in certain circumstances. Having learned many rules of acceptable and unacceptable behaviour, children will often criticise anyone they see breaking the rules:

If we do something wrong, Rebecca, four, is on to us like a ton of bricks and uses the exact same phrases we use with her when she does something wrong, for example, 'Mummy, don't talk with your mouth full', or 'Wash your hands before cooking', and so on.

Georgie, four, often picks us up for doing something wrong, for example, 'Mummy, you crossed the road when the little man was on red – that's naughty', or 'Daddy, you said a rude word'.

As we live with my parents, Jack, five, loves to 'grass me up' to my mum to get me into trouble!

These all-or-none rules are also applied to lying, as children learn that telling lies is bad and telling the truth is good – initially there are no grey areas so they still cannot understand white lies or fibs. Children will therefore tell their parents off for telling a fib, or interrogate them about why they have done it: they need to understand what was done, why it was done and what makes it acceptable (or not) in this particular circumstance. For example, five-year-old Emily and her mother were sitting in a café when a family friend arrived with a birthday present. Her mother unwrapped the gift – a China figurine – and exclaimed how lovely it was. Not understanding the use of a white lie in this situation, Emily protested, 'But you've already got one like that and you said it was disgusting.' Many parents of young children will be familiar with this experience.

> It would be quite difficult to pull off a fib around Ellie, five, as she would be very challenging about it (i.e., interrogating me) if she suspected or found out. She wouldn't be upset, but judgemental.

> Nicola, six, will get confused or upset when she hears me tell a white lie, for example, when I said something but did something else, or if I use an excuse that is not true to leave somewhere without delay.

This black-and-white approach to morality may be a way for children to practise their beliefs and become comfortable with them, before experimenting with a more flexible approach.

> Emily, five, has a strong moral sense, especially if she feels that she or someone else has been told off for something they haven't done or that wasn't their fault. If she's been wrongly accused she is so outraged she will say 'You're not my family any longer', and flounce upstairs slamming every door on the way.

> When I called a driver on the road 'a stupid man', Jack, five, quickly told me off for calling him stupid. Not a nice word, I was told.

Along similar lines, many parents have been caught out – by their own child! – when claiming he or she is younger or older than is truly the case. At four or five years of age, the advantage of such selective lying is lost on the child in question and he is quite likely to inadvertently sabotage his parents' efforts:

> If I were trying not to pay for a ticket and say to Theo, five, 'If the lady asks how old you are, say you're four', he will get upset ('I know that's a lie').

> The worst time was when we went to a theme park and I'd stood in a queue for about an hour and a half with all three kids waiting for Rory and Emily to have a turn on the miniature cars. You had to be five to get on the ride before you could get your 'driving licence'. Emily was not quite five, but of course I said she was. Rory and Emily both piped up with 'But she's/I'm not five, she's/I'm still four!' So we had to leave after all that wait without going on the cars at all. It was extremely difficult trying to explain to them why it was acceptable for me to tell a lie in that situation.

Another typical example occurred when one mother was stopped by the police for not displaying a tax disc. She told the policeman that the application was in the post, but later told her five-year-old daughter, who was with her, that she had forgotten to post the form and that it was still on her desk at home. Her daughter was shocked, especially when her mother tried to explain that the fib was OK because it only stretched the truth slightly and successfully got them out of trouble.

Children's rather rigid rules at this age mean that they do not understand that sometimes, in certain circumstances, it is acceptable – or only a little bit naughty – to conceal the truth and lie. As a result, they may go through quite a striking 'goody goody' stage in which they go out of their way to act properly according to the behaviour that they believe is expected of them. For instance:

Having learned the difference between right and wrong, children sometimes go through a goody goody stage

Kishori, five, is scrupulously honest. She can be rather smug about other people doing wrong, for example, 'Anmika tells lies, I don't'. We have conversations about not hurting animals and she tells me she wants to be a vegetarian when she grows up.

After five years of being pretty bad, Emily has been going through a divinely good stage for about six weeks – giving herself homework, doing immaculate writing, fluent reading, beautiful drawings and cards, getting herself up in the morning and dressing herself, tidying up her room, helping Alice get dressed, offering to bath Alice, and hugging Rory if he gets upset!

The other side of this all-or-none approach is that children will often believe that everything they are told is the truth. Although they may understand that people are capable of deceiving others, once they learn that it is wrong to do this, they often assume that other people, especially adults, tell the truth. Young children are thus easy to fool – they do not spot lies easily, especially when they are inexperienced liars themselves. This of course makes young children very vulnerable, but can also be very endearing:

> A friend of Jack's, five, told him that doing a specific thing was wrong. This specific thing was not wrong at all, actually it was quite fun. But because Jack's friend had told him that he shouldn't do that he took it on board as being the truth.

Bending the rules

As adults, we tell lies all the time – to avoid hurting people's feelings and to get out of situations we want to avoid. We treat certain lies as morally wrong, but our moral code allows for many shades of grey as well as clear instances of right and wrong. As children become more capable liars, they also begin to apply the rules they have learned about right and wrong in subtle ways. They will now begin to tell more convincing fibs, such as blaming someone plausible for a misdemeanour, or will leave out certain aspects of the truth without actually lying. For example:

> Theo, five, likes to please and doesn't like to get things wrong. He wouldn't say 'I broke it' but would say 'It got broken' or 'Someone broke it'.

> Jack, five, finds it great now that his sister is mobile – he can blame any mess, toys on the floor, drinks spilling, etc., on her to get himself out of trouble.

At age five, children think that all lying is wrong

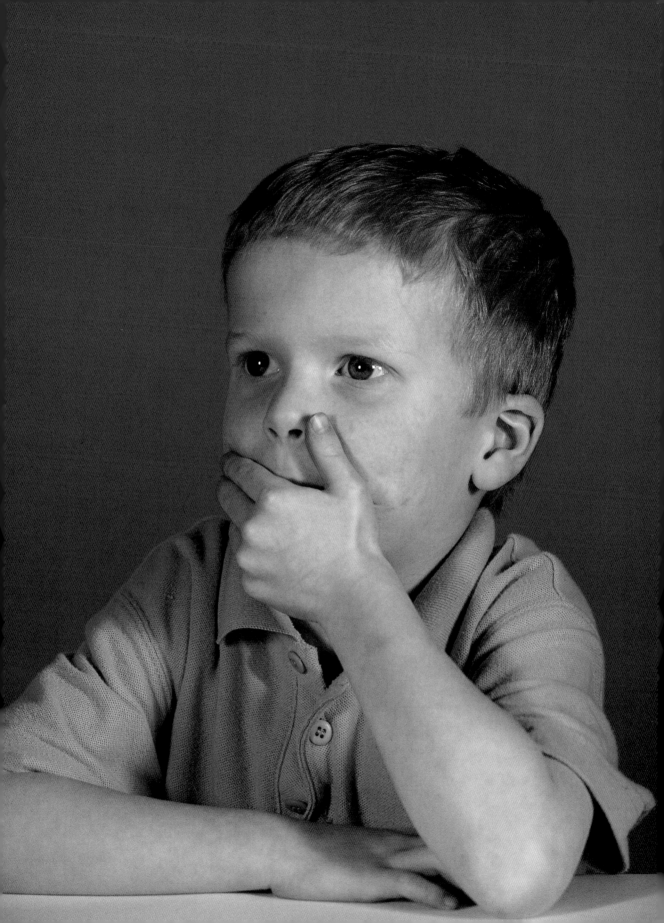

Amanda, six, tells fibs about everything. She kicked her brother first, but she said he did it first – she will always try and pass the buck.

Many children are still living partly in their fantasy world and can tell increasingly imaginative tall stories, of which the following quotations are wonderful examples:

Emily, five, lives in such a fantasy world and is such a convincing liar that it's almost impossible to tell what's truth and what's fantasy/a lie. I have hundreds of examples, but to take two recent ones: she joined a gym class and after about four weeks I was allowed to go in and watch a session. She really fancied the young gym coach and spent much of her time trying to get close to him (she didn't realise I was watching). At the end the coach came up to me and asked if my daughter Kate (!) was always like this, or was it because of the changes at home with her newborn sister, Sarah (no baby!).

Secondly, for the first few weeks of this term, Emily would come home with a note from medical saying that she had had a bad bang on the head in the playground. There never seemed to be any bruises. Then her teacher called me in and said that she'd become aware that when the weather was bad Emily was lying herself down underneath the playground equipment as if she were dead. A playground assistant would come rushing over and Emily would groan that she'd had a terrible fall. The assistant would then have to take her to the nice warm medical room for the rest of playtime! Emily also tells fibs that are easier to spot, for instance she came home the other day and told me that her teacher lived in a lighthouse in the Archway Road with her teenage daughter, Flower.

Theo, seven, makes up stories which I think he half believes himself. He has recently lost several of his baby teeth and he told us that he saw the tooth fairy and that she was wearing a yellow dress. But the next time he lost a tooth, he said that he hadn't seen the fairy again.

In many ways, children are like sponges and continue to absorb a lot of information about acceptable and unacceptable behaviour which they digest and file away for future use. This information helps them constantly to re-evaluate the rules they think operate in the real world and helps them to consolidate their notions of how they – and others – should and should not behave. For example:

Parent: 'Don't do that!'

Nicola, six: 'Well you do it!'

Most parents would be familiar with this dialogue.

Holly, seven, is a bit like the dinosaur in *Toy Story 2* and will pick us up for doing something wrong. Whenever we park she says, 'Are we allowed to park here?' or 'Have you got your seat belt on?' Another one is if I swear and she giggles and says, 'Mummy said the "F" word.'

Alex, six, gets concerned when others are doing things wrong and talks about things he's heard on news items.

As a result, children's rather black-and-white moral thinking now expands to allow for shades of grey. They start to realise that it is sometimes socially acceptable to tell little white lies. They reach this stage by observing the behaviour of those around them and from their increasing sensitivity towards the needs of other people; they are starting to understand the rules of the lying game:

Once or twice the older ones may have heard me lying about their father not being at home if, say, a client he doesn't wish to speak to phones up. Sarah, eight, and Elizabeth, six, have not seemed to bat an eyelid and Jonathan, nine, seems to enjoy the joke.

Corey, seven, doesn't get upset about me telling white lies but he always asks why I have, for example when I have said that we can't go to someone's house as we are busy. I have explained that it is nicer to lie than hurt their feelings by saying you don't want to go.

The lying game

The fact that some lies make people feel good and can be told without punishment helps children understand that it is sometimes acceptable (for example, to spare someone's feelings) to deceive someone into believing that you, the liar, think something you actually do not think. This is a tricky notion for a child to understand partly because it involves an exception to the 'lying is wrong' rule, but it is made even more difficult because telling white lies of this kind is more complex than telling an ordinary lie.

Telling an ordinary lie involves making someone think something that is not true, and children are able to understand this around the age of four. Telling a white lie to spare someone's feelings is more complex because it involves making someone think that you think something that you do not. To understand this, a child must be able to think about thinking – an ability that psychologists call 'second order' theory of mind. For example, if a grandmother gives her grandson a present that he does not like, he may still tell his granny that he really likes it – even if he hates it – in such a way that granny is deceived into believing him. The grandson knows he has lied, but only to be kind. He also understands that, because of the white lie he told, his granny will think that he thinks the present is nice. Children become able to manage this when they are six or seven years of age:

Whenever I give Theo, seven, something he says, 'That's exactly what I wanted' and he sounds like he really means it even if it's a white lie.

Taffy, seven, tells white lies to her friends in order not to hurt their feelings – to get out of play dates, disguising her true feelings over something they might be pleased with, telling other mums she likes their food when she doesn't, etc. She also tries to hoodwink me sometimes, and when she gets caught out she will calmly spin some convoluted tale about how she thought I meant so and so when she was talking about so and so . . .

The other day, Holly, seven, came back from a friend's house saying, 'I didn't like the dinner but I ate it and said it was nice anyway.'

Discovering white lying, and learning how to play the lying game, is an important stage in children's development – it means that children can now understand that other people have their own agendas and may also be hiding and/or faking their true emotions at certain times. This gives children the tools necessary to become suitably suspicious when trying to work out who is being genuine and who is faking. Consequently they are no longer quite so easy to deceive:

If I tell a white lie and say I don't have money to buy toys or things because his father doesn't give his mummy maintenance money, he'll say, 'Then why, Mummy, have you got money to buy me a hot chocolate and cake in a café?' Good point!

If I tell a fib, Taffy, seven, just rolls her eyes to the heavens and murmurs, 'Oh Mummy, you shouldn't tell lies.' (I'm the first to admit I'm a terrible role model!)

Children now have all the skills they need to turn lying into a fine art. They know the difference between good and bad lies and the difference between right and wrong, and they understand that the overlap between the two is not always exact. For example, eight-year-old Danielle and six-year-old Amanda were playing when their mother came in to kiss them goodbye before going out. Doing a little twirl, she asked them how she looked. The girls both said that she looked nice. As soon as the front door had slammed shut, however, the girls started discussing their mother's outfit and confessed that they hated the spots and the colour beige . . . in fact they thought the whole ensemble was horrible. Even so they deliberately told their mother a white lie as they understood that she would otherwise be devastated. Danielle and Amanda can play the lying game. Having had a little more practice than her younger sister, Danielle can even tell quite sophisticated spontaneous white lies:

Danielle, eight, tells white lies to keep everyone happy. She knows her dad thinks chips are bad for her. So when the family were at a motorway service station recently she deliberately chose potatoes not chips because her dad was watching. During the meal her dad went to the loo and Danielle said to her mum, 'Can I have some of your chips because I don't like potatoes?'

Another example is when a Canadian aunt stayed recently. Danielle said to her mum, 'I'd never go to Canada and leave you.' But she said to her aunt, 'I'm saving up to go to Canada so I can be with you.'

Moral reasoning is not yet fully developed, however – it undergoes several more twists and changes between later childhood and adulthood. Around the age of seven, children start to develop strong notions of equality and will believe that everyone should be treated the same, regardless of the circumstances. This belief may stem from their need to prevent complaints, fights or other forms of conflict.

Rory, seven, has a very acute moral sense. He is always talking about the environment and he's very aware of issues like recycling. Many things can upset him – for instance, seeing kids living in poor conditions on the news or beggars in the street – or outrage him, for example if the referee makes a wrong decision at football, or if Emily has one more of anything than him.

As they get older, children start weighing up a variety of different factors when making their moral judgements – including people's differing physical and emotional needs. They may, for example, feel that someone deserves more of something because they are poor or because they are feeling sad or are physically disabled, as if they are trying to impose equality by weighting things in favour of those who find life most challenging. These beliefs seem to shift again from the age of ten onwards when moral judgements become based on both equality and merit, which may involve a quite complex weighing up to ensure everyone gets their just deserts. There is still a tendency to think idealistically rather than realistically, however. For example:

Recently, Amalia, nine, told a member of staff how much she hated her because the person accused her sister of doing something she hadn't. Amalia then demanded the staff member be sacked for lying and asked me how soon she could stop going to the venue. Normally, Amalia and the staff are the best of friends.

Learning how to lie and gaining a sense of fair play are among the most demanding skills we have to acquire en route to the complex world of inequalities, discrimination and hard-won justice in which we have to operate as adults. By the time we reach adulthood, however, we are generally well able to distinguish between right and wrong and understand the moral reasoning that underpins our society. Not only can we hide our true feelings and deliberately deceive another person, we are also sophisticated enough to realise when others want to manipulate us in return. We continue to develop and hone these essential skills until the end of our days – including the ability to tell believable social white lies at dinner parties. We can now play by the rules of the lying game.

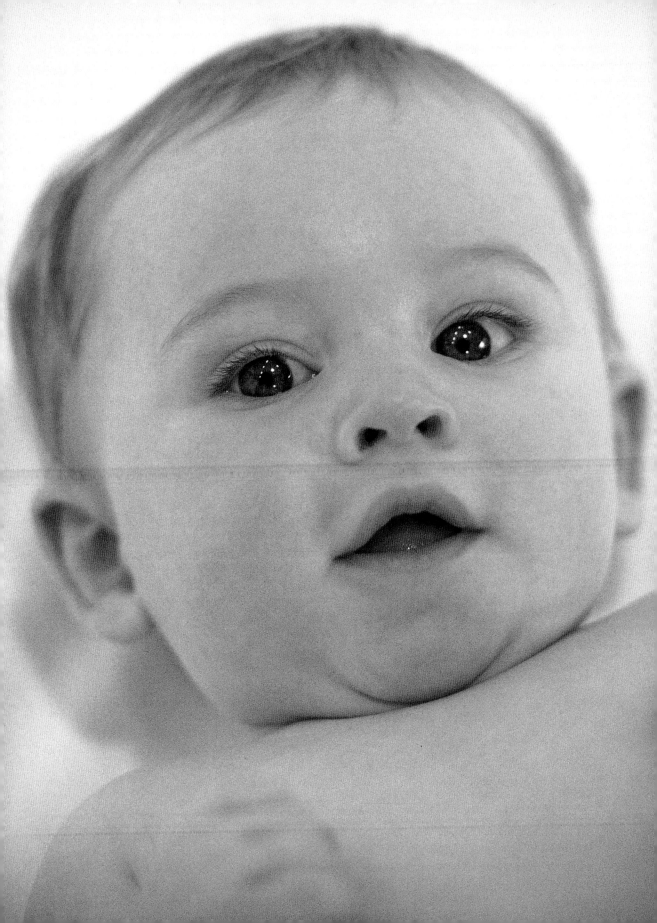

chapter three

the engendered species

'Is it a boy or a girl?' That is usually the first question most of us ask on hearing that a friend or relative has had a new baby. Gender is at the root of one of the most fundamental of all human needs – that of identity. We identify ourselves with those around us on a number of different levels – with our species, our nationality, where we live and most closely with our family and given name. Perhaps our most basic understanding of ourselves as individuals, however, revolves around whether we are male or female. In fact, until we are identified as a boy or girl we are referred to as 'it', and 'its' have no defined place in our society.

As adults, we automatically classify a stranger as either male or female when we meet them. Gender is one of first the things we notice about another person, as the difference between men and women is a key factor in our society. Despite political correctness, the male/female divide is important, and it is obvious all around us – in public toilets, changing cubicles, single-sex hospital wards, advertisements and many shop windows. It is usually obvious in the way we dress, adorn our bodies, style our hair and even in the way we move.

Although we may not realise it, we all view the world through 'gender-coloured' spectacles, which affect our behaviour, the way we think, how we are treated and how we treat others in return. If you have ever mistaken someone's gender, or been mistaken for the opposite sex yourself, you will probably have noticed quite directly the effects that gender has on behaviour.

Gender is an intrinsic part of human identity

Despite the fundamental role that gender plays in our lives, children are not fully aware of this aspect of their identity for several years. Babies are born not knowing that humans fall into two gender groups, never mind which one of those groups they belong to. Children generally know whether they are boys or girls by the age of two, but still do not understand that gender is a permanent and unchanging aspect of their identity. As they grow up, they must also learn about the societal rules associated with gender – from rules as simple as using the appropriate changing room, to the more subtle and complex issues that revolve around gender roles in the home and workplace.

Nature or nurture?

The way our awareness of gender develops is complex – is it inherent in our genes or do we learn it from those around us? The most likely explanation is that it arises from a combination of the two, and that the balance between nature and nurture changes in importance at different stages of our development.

From the moment we are born, our brain is bombarded with gender-related information from the world around us, starting with face shapes, voice pitch, hair styles, height, gait and the colour and shape of people's clothes. Newborn babies have a phenomenal capacity to memorise general information, including the appearance and behaviour of each person they meet. In fact, babies find the human face one of the most fascinating sights in the world and spend a lot of time examining the faces around them. At only one or two months old, babies can discriminate between faces that fit into general categories such as old and young. Experiments even suggest that they can recognise those who are pretty: babies will look longer at faces that are more symmetrical and attractive (as rated by adults) than those we find less attractive. This seems to be an in-born feature rather than one formed by the environment as these babies are too young to have been influenced by learned behaviour. No one knows for certain why this is, but possibly it is some form of survival tactic – symmetry may, for example, indicate stronger, healthier genes when it later comes to selecting a mate.

By the age of three months, the ability to absorb and store information about their surroundings has helped infants to discover the two broad categories of male and female human beings. If a three month old is shown a succession of female faces, he or she soon becomes bored and spends less and less time examining each face. However, if the baby is then shown a different kind of face – a male face – he or she will become alert again and look at the new face for longer. This suggests that, even at this very young age, babies can distinguish between male and female faces.

Although three month olds may be able to spot the difference between male and female faces, they do not yet know what it means. At this stage, babies can only perceive, rather than interpret, what is happening around them and they are programmed to enjoy looking at as many new things as possible in the drive to learn about the fascinating world into which they have been born.

By ten months of age, infants have learned a lot more about each gender. By this age, infants are able to categorise many aspects of the world, and they can recognise patterns of behaviour and other characteristics which are associated with each gender. For example, a baby may notice that the adult males in her life (her father and his friends, her uncles and grandfathers, etc.) tend to have more square-cut features, deeper voices, flat chests and shorter, more receding hair. She may also notice that this type of person tends to wear particular clothes: trousers, sweaters, suits and shirts. She may even have spotted that her daddy has a clean-shaven smooth face when leaving the house in the morning but is bristly on returning in the evening, and that some males have more distinctive facial hair groomed into moustaches or beards. In contrast, the main females in her life (her mother and her friends, her aunts and grannies, etc.) will tend to have oval faces with softer features, more brightly coloured lips, make-up defined eyes, a higher-pitched voice and more flowing hair, along with a face that is always hairless. These people will also tend to have softer, different-shaped bodies and wear more colourful clothes that often expose their lower legs, arms and upper chest.

Infants soon notice patterns among the many voices, faces, hair patterns, gaits and behavioural patterns that they have seen and may become quite confused if these appear to contradict each other. In an experimental situation, for example, babies will look much longer at an adult who appears to have characteristics that fit into both gender categories, such as a male face with a female voice, than at an adult whose voice and face match in terms of gender. The cues that infants use to determine gender are surprisingly subtle – if a male face is presented with a female voice that has been artificially pitch-shifted to make it sound more like that of a male, infants still seem to be able to tell that it is really a female voice and not that of a male.

By the age of twelve months a child is aware of the gender of others and will react differently to the faces of males and females. Some infants do so even earlier, as the following quotation shows:

> As a baby, Elizabeth didn't like men, including her father, and would cry continually if he (or for that matter any man) was in the same room as her. This started at around four to five months old and lasted until she was well over one year old.

Around this time, even though they have no sense of the gender to which they belong, infants start to show signs of male or female behaviour themselves. If a group of one-year-old infants are in nappies, or dressed identically, their sex is often revealed purely by the items they choose to play with. When offered a selection of toys, girls spend more time playing with dolls and cuddly animals, while boys show a preference for more traditionally masculine items such as plastic tools, lorries, cars and tractors. For example:

> Holly, one, is already into dollies and cuddly toys, much more than Jack, five, ever was at this age.

> We have noticed a big difference between boys and girls. Joss, one, likes to push cars or trains along the floor and building towers while Suzanna, three, role plays with dolls and 'babies' although we don't treat them differently.

Girls like Carmen, eighteen months, are often attracted to traditionally feminine toys, even before they fully understand their own gender

Surprisingly, children develop a preference for sex-stereotyped toys months before they can identify their own sex. This sex-stereotyped behaviour becomes stronger with age, so that an eighteen-month-old boy may, for example, sit on a vacuum cleaner making car noises – boy-like behaviour – before he is even aware that he is a boy.

Why is this? No one really knows. Gender development certainly begins in the womb, and the sex hormones that stimulate development of the reproductive organs may influence areas of the brain to develop in a more typically masculine or feminine way. All embryos will develop into girl babies unless the male hormone, testosterone, is present – hence boys have nipples, although they do not actually need them. Testosterone has a profound effect on the development of male physical characteristics and is now thought to help shape the male mind too.

Testosterone seems to affect brain development so that male brains are physically distinct from female brains in several ways. The most obvious difference occurs where the two halves of the brain – the left and right hemispheres – communicate with each other through a large bundle of nerves known as the corpus callosum. In boys, fewer cross-connections

Boys tend to enjoy more physical play...

...and they are often interested in finding out how things work

develop between the two hemispheres, so the communicating corpus callosum is significantly smaller than in girls. At the same time, the right hemisphere in male brains forms more internal connections within itself and therefore works more independently in males than in females. As a result, boys seem to tackle some types of problem using only one side of their brain, while girls use both the left and right sides. This may explain why boys tend to be more interested and proficient in right-sided brain activities such as mathematics and spatial tasks, such as taking things apart to find out how they work. For example:

James, three, wants to know how everything works. He is obsessed with holes in the road, building works and building equipment.

Oliver, two, loves trains, tractors and building machines. He likes taking apart his toys and trying to put them back together.

ABOVE: Even at this young age, boys' brains are significantly different to girls'

LEFT: Two year old Tré's boisterous behaviour is influenced by his male hormones

The influence of testosterone also produces more aggressive or assertive behaviour in boys, even as infants, as illustrated by the following observation:

> Our son, two, is louder, pushier, more assertive and must always come first even if it means using his physical ability. Our daughter wants to be noticed and praised more for her good behaviour.

The influence of male hormones before birth suggests that nature plays a major role in the development of gender roles. It is likely that children are born with a bias towards male or female behaviour depending on whether or not they were exposed to testosterone in the womb. However, this is not the whole story. Nurture, or experience and up-bringing, is also a major influence. Children may be born with an innate bias towards male or female behaviour, but this bias is almost certainly enhanced or diminished by their experience of the outside world where they are bombarded with a multitude of gender-related cues.

Once adults know the sex of a baby, they begin to impose their own gender stereotypes on the baby, often quite subconsciously. Even when they are just twenty-four hours old, baby boys tend to be described as stronger, hardier and better co-ordinated than baby girls, who are perceived as softer, delicate and more awkward. This happens even with male and female babies who are the same weight and height and have the same physical score at birth! Words such as handsome and strapping are used to described boys, while more feminine terms such as pretty and cute are used to describe girls.

Even parents who have decided not to impose gender-specific toys, clothes and colours on their offspring still give many subtle cues that encourage sex-stereotypical behaviour and help to shape their children's attitudes and behaviour – whether they mean to or not. For example, observational studies suggest that adults tend to hold boys and girls differently, talk to girls more and indulge boys in more rough and tumble play. If a girl falls over she is more likely to be hugged and comforted, while a boy is more likely to be ignored or encouraged not to fuss:

With the girls, Danielle, eight, Amanda, six, and Natasha, two, if they fall and hurt themselves I would cuddle them for longer than I would with my son Bradley, four. I would give him a quick cuddle and say 'You're OK, off you go.'

I invariably treat my daughters, Anmika, seven, and Kishori, five, differently from my son, Jashan, three, although I try not to. I think I give my son less attention when he hurts himself, but then again he makes less fuss.

James, three, is much more rough and boisterous than Eleanor, five, and I am much firmer with James as he is so boisterous, but also more affectionate as he demands it.

'Isn't she a sweetie!' Adults will often use different language when describing male and female infants

Parents tend subconsciously to encourage male children
to be tougher than girls

The above quotations illustrate differences in the way parents treat their sons and daughters. Although parents are partly responding to differences in behaviour that already exist in their offspring, they also play a role in creating these differences. Jashan naturally fusses less than his sisters when he hurts himself, so his parent pays less attention; not paying much attention in turn encourages Jashan not to fuss and to be self sufficient if he does trip over.

Less subtly, parents tend to reinforce gender roles in their offspring by buying them particular toys and clothes; dolls and pink clothes for girls, tractors and blue clothes for boys. In other situations, parental cues about behaviour may be more overt, as in this example:

When Saxon, four, recently appeared downstairs wearing a pink sweatshirt and bracelet belonging to his cousin, both his mother and his granny insisted he take them off – we both felt distinctly uncomfortable with his girlish appearance, especially as guests were due!

Parents and other adults also give children clues about what is 'right' and 'wrong' gender behaviour by the way they react when watching children play with certain toys, particularly with boys. Parents, especially fathers, are likely to disapprove when boys show girlish behaviour, although tomboyish behaviour may be quite acceptable in girls.

Overall, both nature and nurture are important in determining gender-specific behaviour. There *are* biological differences between boys and girls that extend beyond the obvious physical differences and influence behaviour. At the same time, there are clear differences in the way adults *treat* boys and girls. But the two processes interact: parents respond to biologically based differences and their responses are likely to reinforce certain behaviours while diminishing others. In many ways, it is perhaps the interaction between nature and nurture, rather than one or the other, that is most important in determining a given child's development.

Which one am I?

Children learn to call themselves boys or girls as a result of being given these labels by adults. From day one, children hear the terms 'boy' or 'girl' applied to them, often many times a day, in phrases such as 'clever girl' or 'good boy'. This information is filed away and almost as soon as they are able to talk, children can say whether they are girls or boys. If an adult mistakenly identifies a child as the wrong sex the child will quickly – sometimes quite angrily – point out the mistake. Boys are often particularly sensitive to misidentification, as the following quotation shows:

If I say to Aaron, two, by mistake 'Good girl' he says, 'Silly Mummy, I'm not a girl, I'm a boy.'

This is not to say that two year olds understand what being a boy or girl actually means, however. Far from it. At this stage the word is just a label. Children simply recognise which label applies to them in the same way they have learned to recognise their own names. Children of this age may also notice that people have different genitals:

Holly, eighteen months, knows she's different from her brother Jack, five, and finds boys' bits fascinating in the bath.

Aaron, two, knows he's got a willy like his brother, Theo, while Holly has got a space. He says Mummy has got a hairy bottom and he knows boys do standing up wees and girls sit down.

Ewan can see he and Mia are not exactly the same

Oliver, two, knows that he has a willy and Daddy has a willy, but Mummy doesn't. He also knows that Mummy has 'boobies' but he doesn't – he just accepts it as fact.

At this stage, penises and vaginas are just categorised like short and long hair, trousers and dresses: they are simply features that some people have and some people do not. Children initially have no idea that genitals denote gender in a biological sense and it takes them a little while to work out who has what, as these quotations show:

Maxim, two, is very aware of his willy and has been for over six months. He talks about it a lot. He recently asked me if I had a willy and I explained to him that women don't have willies. I'm not sure he fully understood because he says 'MacMac [his name for himself] has willy, Theo [his brother] has willy, Fabi [another brother] has willy, Daddy has willy . . .' And then, 'Grandma has willy?'

Helena, two, is aware of the differences between girls and boys. She is very sure that boys wear pants and girls wear knickers, but has asked why she hasn't got a willy.

When Philip, three, and Sarah, four, were in the bath, Philip asked, 'How do you know Sarah's a girl and I'm a boy? Is it because I have my hair cut?'

Joshua, three, recently asked his mother, 'Where's your willy? Under your hairs?'

Leon, four, said to me, 'Boys have dickies. Has your dickie fallen or broken off, Mummy?'

As they approach the age of three, most children can identify correctly children of the same sex as themselves from photographs, labelling them as either boys or girls and using visual clues such as face shape, hair length and style as well as clothing and jewellery (or lack of it). Interestingly, once they can do this, they are more likely to select children of their own gender to play with. Their emerging understanding of gender now strongly influences their behaviour, but currently no theory can adequately explain how infants' preferences for certain toys and behaviours start to form as early as one year of age, before they even know the gender group to which they belong.

Who does what?

Males and females generally behave differently and have different roles in society. Young children show preferences for different types of toys before they are aware of the differences between male and female, as described earlier, but they also learn about typically male and female behaviour from watching adults and other children around them. From the age of two, as soon as they start to understand that there is a difference between the two genders, children start to pick up on conventions and 'rules' about 'what boys do' and 'what girls do'.

By the age of three, children are able to identify themselves clearly as boys or girls and are beginning to develop a better understanding of what this actually means. Notions of 'what boys do' and 'what girls do' become personally relevant, rather than just being examples of 'what other people do'. Children now begin to work out rules about how they think boys and girls should behave, and may apply these rules in a very rigid all or none way as they attempt to create a clear distinction between boys and girls. At this stage there is no flexibility in their thinking, so strong is the urge to create clear-cut rules. Something is either 'a boy thing' or 'a girl thing', so a preschool child's pronouncements can often sound very sexist! For example:

James, three, has quite chauvinist ideas which I find disturbing.

Leon, four, often says thinks like: 'This is only a boys' thing', or 'This is not for girls', 'Girls do different things than boys' and once, 'Only boys go in spaceships'.

Alex, four, says that girls like pink and wear skirts and have long hair.

Children apply these gender-related rules to themselves, too, using them to govern everything from clothing and toys to ways of behaving. The following quotations are typical of gender appreciation in action:

When my grandson, Alexander, was nearly three, he had a beautiful head of curls. He insisted that his mother get them cut off, however so he would 'look like a proper boy'. Recently, aged four-and-a-half, he threw a fit about wearing tights (it got very cold) – 'No, no, no, only girls wear tights!' So he had cold legs in socks all day. His younger brother, Misha, was happy to wear tights.

Sophie, four, thinks girls should only wear pink. Buying clothes can be a real headache, because she simply won't wear things that aren't pink!

Sabrina, age three, wants pink everything

Rio, fifteen months, is starting to understand that the model train
is the 'appropriate' gender toy for him

Rebekah, three, doesn't like me to wear Daddy's shirts or tee-shirts.

My son Akira, four, doesn't like to wear anything that is for girls.

The application of gender rules is often seen clearly when young children
are given a selection of toys to play with. If a little girl is given a doll, a toy
truck and something more neutral, such as toy animals, she will often
stare at the toys at first. But this is not simply a blank stare – one theory
of gender development suggests that she is carefully appraising each toy
and deciding whether, according to her rules, it is a toy for a girl or a boy.
Once she has decided, she will choose the toy that is relevant for her own
gender and select the doll to play with.

Learning the roles

Once children have grasped the concept of gender, they begin to interpret the world according to what they know about each gender's characteristics and behaviour patterns. By the age of three, having established their own gender identity, children usually show an increased interest in objects and activities that are associated with their own gender. Social learning and adult role models are important in this process; children learn the appropriate behaviour for their gender by observing how a large number of males and females behave. The earliest learning about gender roles, especially in two-parent families, often comes from imitating the actions and activities of their same sex parent.

Imitation, and in particular adult responses to children's imitation, subtly shapes young children's behaviour and teaches them about gender-appropriate behaviour. Boys identify with Daddy – the 'big boy' in a family – and tend to be encouraged and praised when they copy Daddy's behaviour. Little girls likewise imitate Mummy and are rewarded with smiles and attention for doing so. A three-year-old boy, for example, will happily pretend to use a spanner and hammer like Daddy, while a little girl may tend to her doll in the same way she has seen Mummy nursing a baby. Mothers, fathers, grandparents, childminders, family friends, aunts, uncles and older siblings all act as role models, and the range of activities that children learn to copy is wide:

Ewan, three, likes to swear and spit like Daddy and pretends to smoke a cigarette.

Sammy, three, likes copying his daddy, while Naomi, five, copies me – especially my shouting!

Abigail, three, imitates me by playing Mummy, feeding her baby doll and pretending to cook and iron.

Bradley, four, imitates his grandfather by getting his plastic tools and fixing furniture.

Rebekah, three, likes dancing and copies dancers off the TV. She says 'I'm a girl' quite a lot, but isn't overly feminine yet. She likes putting on lipstick or other make-up if she sees me putting it on. She doesn't like dresses and goes crazy if I try to put her into one. I don't wear them, so I guess she won't like them either.

Rebecca, four, does seem to imitate me. She likes to take her time choosing her clothes, brushing her hair and loves long baths like me. When she's playing and talking to her toys in role play she is the mother. She tells them off like I tell her off. She pretends to have a baby and it is always a girl. Occasionally, if it is a boy, she says 'Mummy, I've had a baby boy. You can have it.'

Interestingly, children seldom become fascinated by the personal grooming rituals of their opposite sex parent – probably because such behaviour is discouraged by the reaction they receive. Daddy may gladly show his young son how to shave but shoos his daughter away, telling her that shaving is something that girls don't do. Similarly, Mummy may happily apply a little lipstick to her young daughter's lips while telling her son it is not appropriate:

When Saxon was three he always asked to put on lipstick when watching me make up in the mornings. At first, I put a little on him, but then felt guilty and refused to do this any more, telling him he couldn't have any because he was a boy.

The above quote is a lovely example of social learning in action, highlighting the fact that, as parents, we teach our children gender-stereotyped behaviour based on the social conventions we take for granted in adult life.

By the age of three, children also start to assign jobs to gender, based on the roles played by the adults they have observed. For example:

Trimane, three, believes that daddies go to work and that mummies look after children.

Isaac and Mathew, both three, are fascinated by the monster truck

> My daughter Georgie, four, has fixed ideas that mummies drive cars, fix hair, brush teeth, while daddies do shoulder rides, tickles, etc.

> Ellie, five, connects women with being mummies but also with working in a child-orientated environment, for example being a teacher. She connects men with being at work, out of the house.

Children aged around four still find it difficult to apply two different concepts to a single situation. Although they are beginning to understand that it is possible to represent something in more than one way, they still have trouble doing just that. As a result, four year olds sometimes cannot understand that males and females have many different but simultaneous roles in life. A mother can be both Mummy and a doctor, for example, but not in the eyes of her four year old! Young children still getting to grips with multiple roles sometimes deny that they are possible:

> We have a woman doctor in the family and Craig said that she can't be a doctor because she's a girl. That was a while ago, so hopefully that's changed.

Once a girl, always a girl . . .

Even though children of three and four years of age are beginning to grasp social conventions about how boys or girls – including themselves – should act and dress, they are still unaware that gender is stable: they know they are boys or girls, but they do not realise that they have always been the same gender and always will be. A three-year-old girl may think she was once a baby boy, for example, particularly if all the babies she knows happen to be boy babies. Similarly, she will be unaware that she will always be a girl and will grow up to become a woman, as the following quotations illustrate:

> Amy, three, recently said, 'When I'm bigger I'll be like Daddy.'

> My son Jashan, three, refuses to wear tights until he is a 'big girl'.

> When he was four, Fabian was surprised when he noticed that a girl friend of his didn't have a willy. When I said, 'Of course she doesn't have a willy, she's a girl,' he replied, 'I thought girls had willies when they were children and they lost them when they grew up.'

These children have not yet grasped the concept that gender is stable over time – that girl babies become little girls, who become women, and boy babies become boys, who become men. By four, children realise this, but still do not fully understand the constancy of gender, and tend to assume that people's gender depends on their appearance. They believe it is possible to swap sex as easily as changing clothes. A three-year-old girl may happily believe, for instance, that she can turn her baby brother into a girl merely by putting him into a pink frilly dress.

> I was confident that Saxon, four, knew that if he put on a dress he wouldn't turn into a girl. But when I asked him, he said quite matter of factly that putting on a dress meant he would turn into a girl, 'You silly'.

> Alex, four, had a long tee-shirt on the other day and burst into tears because he was petrified that someone would think he was a girl.

These four year olds can be easily confused by the gender signals given out by outward appearance. Thus a person with long hair who is wearing a dress is seen as female, while someone with short hair who is wearing a tie is seen as a male. If these same people were to change into different clothes and alter their hair style to look like the other sex, children who did not understand gender constancy would say that the people had changed sex.

A large part of the problem for young children is that they are unable to understand that appearance can be misleading, which often happens in the case of gender. Not until they are around four or five years old can children make what psychologists call the 'appearance–reality distinction'. At this age, children begin to understand that people have their own minds and thus can have different perspectives or views about given events, as described in Chapter 1. At the same time, children realise that they themselves can have more than one view about the same event. Once they understand this, they are able to understand that a single object or event can appear one way and in reality be somewhat different. In other words, children can make the appearance–reality distinction and can grasp the fact that two different representations (the appearance and the reality) can simultaneously apply to a single thing.

Children who cannot make this distinction tend to assume that appearance equals reality – so if a person looks like a girl, then they are a girl. Of course this does not just apply to gender. A classic test of children's ability to distinguish between appearance and reality involves making a dog look like a cat. In this test a child sits in front of a small stage and the curtains are drawn back to reveal a man with a real, live dog. The experimenter introduces the dog, 'This is Chico', and asks, 'What is Chico?' The child will, of course, say, 'He's a dog.' The experimenter then explains, 'We're going to play a little game with Chico', and puts a cat mask on the dog. The child is then asked, 'What does Chico look like, a cat or a dog?' and will, as expected, say, 'A cat!' The experimenter then asks the child 'What is Chico really, a cat or a dog?' Children under the age of four typically reply that Chico is really a cat, as long as the cat mask is on the dog. At this age, children seem to believe that the identity of the animal has actually changed to match his external appearance, so Chico has effectively turned into a cat. From about four years of age, however, children understand that, despite the mask, Chico is still a dog. Children who grasp this concept are also able to understand that gender remains constant, regardless of appearance:

> Tavey, four, knows he's a boy but will pretend to be a girl. He knows that he isn't really, even if he's dressed up.

> Jack, five, knows that just because he puts on a dress or skirt that it won't make him into a little girl.

Comparing genitals is an important step towards finally realising what gender is and that it is permanent. Most children develop a fascination with genitalia at some stage as this is the most obvious external evidence of the biological difference between males and females. Children as young as two notice differences in genitals, but by four years of age they have worked out what this means and how it relates to each gender. For example:

> My twin girls, Francesca and Sicily, four, say that boys have willies and girls have 'privates'.

> My daughter Georgie, four, is fascinated by male genitalia, but rarely talks about it – just has a damn good look! She seems to take it for granted that boys have something different to girls.

> When asked how she knew she was a girl, Abigail, three, said she doesn't have a willy.

> Ewan, three, and Alex, four, both know that boys have willies and girls don't, but they haven't yet asked why!

When children reach this last stage of gender identity development, they finally realise that gender is constant across all time and all situations and that they belong to one particular group. They will know that boys grow up to be men and that girls grow up to be women and have babies. The following quotations illustrate how children of this age are starting to think:

> Theo, five, understands men and women are different and says, 'Men are stronger but not really different except to look at. They wear different clothes and men don't have babies and they don't have spaces [vaginas] and they have short hair.'

> Nicola, six, knows that babies come from mummies' (not daddies') tummies.

This final understanding about gender permanence depends partly on an important shift in the way children think. Thinking that is largely intuitive and based on children's immediate perceptions of the world, is now replaced by a more logical way of viewing the world. Children's understanding of reality has advanced and is more abstract. They now understand that some aspects of the world around them can appear superficially different at times yet essentially remain permanent and unchanging underneath. As such, children become able to rely on what they know rather than on what they perceive, and they understand that gender (among many other things) stays the same, no matter what happens.

The difference between a child who understands that gender is constant and a child who does not know this can be striking. For example, in today's world, children may well come across men and women who are dressed in non-stereotypical fashion – such as a man with long, flowing hair, dressed in a flowery pink sarong. To a three to four year old, such a person is obviously a woman, since 'she' is dressed as such. A six year old, however, knows that the person is a man, even though he looks more like a woman. If the children were to see the man in question take off his sarong to reveal shorts and a male physique, the six year old would not be surprised; the three year old, on the other hand, would stare, eyes open in amazement, as the 'woman' transforms into a man!

Playing together: them and us

As children begin to socialise and play regularly with other children, they often show clear preferences for same-sex peers and certain styles of play. Gender segregation along these lines sometimes starts from as early as two years of age and is usually established by the age of three. Girls and boys are especially likely to separate into same-sex groups when children are left to their own devices and allowed to select their own playmates. This suggests that the driving force behind gender segregation in play comes from the children themselves rather than from the adults who supervise them. The following quotations are typical:

Abigail, three, only has girls as playmates. She has recently decided she does not like boys.

I let James, three, and Eleanor, five, choose their own playmates and they have friends of both sexes though predominantly the same sex as themselves.

Even at the age of eighteen months, girls and boys tend to prefer to play with children of the same sex

My daughter Georgie, four, says that boys are generally naughty and she feels girls are infinitely superior although she does have a couple of special boy friends.

There are at least two potential explanations for this almost instinctive tendency for girls and boys to prefer playing with same-sex peers at this age. It is likely that early sex hormones influence children's styles of play. Differences between male and female behaviour are believed to be related to the way sex hormones affect the parts of the brain involved in personality and aggression. Boys also have different energy levels and stronger muscles than girls, which enable them to take part in more boisterous activity. But these differences between the sexes are also self perpetuating – the more muscles are used and exercised, the bigger and stronger they grow.

Probably as a result of these biological differences, little boys' play tends to be rougher and more physical, involving a lot of movement. Girls tend to show calmer, quieter styles of play. This difference is clear even when children are very young. Once children start to play together, they tend to choose play partners whose style of play suits their own – which automatically leads to a degree of segregation between boys and girls. Girls may find boys' more active, boisterous and physically aggressive play rather overwhelming, for example, and thus prefer to play with other girls. Likewise, boys may avoid girls because they find them too passive, inactive and quiet.

A second possible explanation for gender segregation in play relates to learning about gender roles. One theory about how children learn gender-specific behaviour is that, once they understand they are permanently either male or female, they become motivated to learn more about that particular gender as it has become directly relevant to themselves. This does not explain the gender-specific behaviour observed before children really understand that their gender is constant, but may help to explain why school-aged children tend to associate only with members of their own sex.

Six-year-old Joshua's sense of identity is strengthened by playing with friends of the same sex

Of course, these explanations need not be mutually exclusive. Preferring to play with children who have similar styles of play and wanting to learn more about your own gender may both contribute to the gender segregation that is commonly seen among young children.

By the age of four, it has been estimated that children spend three times as much time interacting with children of the same sex than of the opposite sex. By the age of six, the amount of time children spend playing with friends of the same sex is typically ten times greater than that spent with the opposite gender. Some studies of older children, aged eight to eleven, even suggest that half of them spend no time at all interacting with classmates of the opposite sex. At this stage of development the male/female divide is therefore more pronounced compared with just a few years earlier. For example:

Anmika, seven, thinks boys can be silly and refuse to play nicely, just wanting to run about all the time. Since being in a single-sex classroom this year for the last two months, she says she doesn't miss the boys at all.

Khalil, seven, largely has boys as playmates. He has no real opinions about the opposite sex, but has observed that some girls in his class are bossy or naughty. He is a little bit in awe of girls, I think.

This is quite embarrassing, but Taffy, eight, has said that men are quite useless and dopey. I know that's awful but I come from a fiercely matriarchal family where the women sit around talking like characters in an Alan Bennett play and she no doubt is heading the same way.

Jonathan, nine, has friends who are almost exclusively boys, Sarah, eight, has exclusively girl friends while the younger children, Elizabeth, six, and Helena, two, have a mix of friends from both sexes.

Four year olds like Francesca and Sicily will often profess to hate children of the opposite sex, preferring to spend time with groups of friends of their own gender

In fact, children will not just choose to spend time with the same gender, but will often go out of their way to avoid those of the opposite sex, splitting into groups and even hurling abuse at one another. This is not because they actually hate each other, even if they say they do, but because interacting positively with the opposite sex in front of their same-sex peers is to risk being seen as less 'male' or less 'female' and therefore less acceptable to their own group:

Max, nine, hates girls and won't have any to play or to his party. He accepts that the sisters of his friends come to play here, but even though he does talk to them a bit he won't admit it. His brother Corey, seven, doesn't like girls either which is probably caused by Max, who laughs at him if he gets invited to a girl's party.

Sasha, ten, and Tara, four, hate boys except their brother, Nick, who is eight.

Interestingly, however, this behaviour tends to occur at the group level rather than at the individual level, and children who will ignore a friend of the opposite sex when their same-sex peers are around may play happily with that same friend at home:

> Finlay, six, mainly plays with Lego but when girls are around he is very proud to offer them a good play with Mummy's old Barbies and is very disappointed if they don't show excitement about it. He also likes playing mummies and daddies. He seems to thoroughly enjoy these games with girls, but wouldn't dream of playing them with his male friends – or even suggesting it!

> My son Georgie, seven, tends to stick with male friends but is very popular with the girls. Often, he's the only boy invited to the girls' parties. He has been teased by his older brother Harry, eleven, about the girls' interest in him and can be a bit defensive if he feels there's any possibility of teasing.

The two quotations above also reflect the fact that same-sex peer groups are very important in the development of gender roles and gender-stereotyped behaviour. Same-sex peers positively reinforce one another playing in a gender-typical manner by joining in, laughing and praising each other. Any gender-inappropriate play is often frowned upon, criticised or even flatly rejected in a same-sex peer group, especially among boys. Once the sexes have segregated into two groups, their styles of play and behaviour become even more differentiated and stereotyped, as they reinforce each other's perceptions of how males and females should behave.

Girls tend to play more quietly in smaller groups, or stand around chatting. They typically develop one or two close 'best' friends with whom they have equal status and will go out of their way to avoid conflict. Girls bond with other girls through talking, sharing secrets and forming close emotional ties.

> Sarah, eight, and friends talk about clothes, boys and pop music. Other times they prepare a 'show' for everyone to watch and get very involved in the characters they are creating.

In contrast, boys tend to hang around in larger groups and indulge in rough and tumble horseplay. Boys are also more likely to resolve conflicts through physical means and settle differences with their fists. Male friendships are more likely to be based on shared activities and interests, such as sport, rather than being underpinned by sharing emotional confidences.

> Jonathan, nine, and friends talk sports results, who is best at whatever and about Harry Potter. Introductions to new friends are made by way of 'What football club do you support?'

Boys are also more likely to show pack behaviour, going around in groups with a few select males asserting themselves, competing with each other and displaying dominant behaviour. Boys often need a defined hierarchy to feel secure, which is one reason why they tend to form gangs, which bring a sense of order, belonging and safety. For girls, however, this is less of a concern and if they feel insecure they are more likely to back away than to jostle and make a lot of noise. As children grow older, differences between male and female behaviour become increasingly marked, as effectively summed up by the following quotations:

> I only have boys, Kaspar, nine, and Max, seven, but I feel that boys are more action and movement and girls are better focused and concentrated.

> Rowan, eleven, and other boys seem a little more chaotic, messy and perhaps less focused on what they wish to achieve than girls. They tend to be more centred on themselves. They also seem more fragile in some ways – it's tough trying to develop into a twenty-first-century male!

Older children also continue to copy the behaviour of their main same-sex role models as they conform to the behaviour expected of their own gender. For instance:

> Khalil, seven, imitates his father in tone of voice, facial expressions and posture.

Twin girls Amalia and Tsehai, nine, both copy Mum, especially when telling each other off – hands on hips, etc., repeating certain terms I've used.

Billy, ten, and Becky, seven, both copy their same-sex parent. Becky will help dust with polish and want to clean out things. Billy likes to help with gardening and DIY jobs.

The engendered species

Despite their early lack of flexibility about anything involving gender, there comes a time when children start to appreciate that gender rules don't have to be rigid and can often be bent when appropriate. This is well illustrated by a simple example involving a boy helping his mother sweep the kitchen floor at various stages of childhood. At age two, he is happy to help his mother sweep up as he loves to imitate and wants to copy her. From the age of three or four, however, he may refuse to sweep as it goes against his gender rules and he may regard sweeping as a job for girls rather than for boys. By the age of eight, however, he may be happy to help his mum sweep up again as he begins to realise that the rules he has acquired about gender (in this case that only girls use brooms) are only conventions and not strict rules.

This shift in thinking usually begins around the age of seven when children learn to reason more flexibly and start to realise that their strict gender-related rules do not completely work in the real world they are experiencing. They now understand that girls can do boy things and vice versa. Mummies can be doctors, soldiers and business executives, while daddies can be nurses, secretaries and house husbands. As children grow older, they therefore begin to relax their gender stereotypes, as the following quotations show:

Holly, seven, says boys can be sweet, too. They can do the same things as girls.

As children grow older, they start to be more flexible about
traditional gender roles

Becky, nine, thinks of women as being the ones who spend the most
time with their kids, but also knows that women and men can be in
basically any profession. For example, her doctor and dentist are
women, her mum is an attorney, as are the mothers of two of her best
friends, but her last few elementary school teachers have been men.

Jonathan, nine, and Sarah, eight, believe that women look after
children, wash, cook, clean, etc., and that men go out to work and
play football. Interestingly, however, the types of jobs they feel are
open to men and women are interchangeable; men and women can
be doctors, police, nurses, etc.

Learning that gender roles are actually very flexible gives children a new-found confidence in their judgements about the world and helps them make more mature observations such as the following:

> A boy at school said it was sissy to play with girls. My son Taliesin, nine, however, told him that half the world is made up of girls and that he would have trouble when he got older if he didn't learn to get on with them.

> Mary, nine, is very sensitive to inequalities and is quick to charge, for example, radio presenters with sexism.

> Aisha, ten, thinks women should go out to work as well as men and both come back and share the washing up and other household chores.

> Aleishia, twelve, understands that it is not only men who can achieve things and that anything men can do, women can do the same.

Understanding gender flexibility also gives children of both sexes the confidence to start embracing opposite-sex friendships. In the play ground environment they may still feel more confident in same-sex groups, but outside this, children begin to be more flexible in their friendship. For example:

> My son Harry, eleven, has a girl as a best friend, although she is a tomboy. They have a foursome, two boys and two girls, who hang out together.

> Jonathan, nine, comments that the girls in his class are 'nice' and 'clever' and his 'friends' but not his 'girlfriends'. Sarah, eight, wonders if boys 'fancy' her and gets embarrassed when talking about the boys she thinks are good looking.

Similarly, this change in thinking may allow children to feel comfortable getting involved in activities which are non-stereotypical, for example:

Taffy, eight, has never been into dolls but she adores soft toys and
will spend hours making up games with them. She also rummages
around in our bins (which drives me to distraction) and squirrels
away junk that she then transforms into some sort of machine.
She likes to hang out with her father in the garage and create things
out of wood and metal.

As they move into adolescence, children's understanding of gender is
complex and flexible. They have come a long way from lying in their cots
and noticing that there are distinct differences in the faces, hair styles,
sounds and mannerisms of those peering in to smile and coo at them!
Girls and boys now have all the tools they need to fit into the engendered
world to which they belong. The rigid rules that constrain the behaviour
of younger children are gone, replaced by a more flexible understanding
of male and female roles. As adolescents, children will find their own roles,
and it will not be long before they discover that the opposite sex does,
after all, have its own biological attractions!

chapter four

the thinker

'Cogito, ergo sum' – I think, therefore I am – stated the French philosopher Descartes. Descartes was debating whether he could prove that he actually existed, but he also managed to capture in that simple phrase one of the most essential aspects of being human. As adults we are thinking all the time. During the space of a single minute, more thoughts than we can count go through our heads. These may revolve around common, every-day events such as planning a menu and writing a shopping list or relate to more complex tasks such as planning a route and dealing with unexpected diversions when driving.

In this situation, the driver may have a route planned but then may have to change it unexpectedly, while still driving, taking note of road signs, considering different route options, holding them in mind, comparing them for their length (in distance and in time) and deciding which to take. That is in addition to the business of driving the car itself, considering suggestions from any passengers, possibly following verbal directions and maybe even singing along to the radio!

As adults, we can manage all this with astonishing ease. We know that the world follows certain rules. We understand simple laws of physics and can interpret signs, symbols and writing – often in more than one language. We are capable of thinking ahead, of imagining possibilities and of making plans upon which we can act, as well as weighing up different options and making appropriate choices. In short, we have impressive powers of thinking and reasoning that we use almost continuously to make sense of the world.

Thinking intelligently is a fundamental part of human nature

One of the most important aspects of our thinking ability is our capacity to think about things that we are not actually in contact with, or situations that have not yet happened or that happened in the past. We can think about real objects, people and events, but we can also think about things that are not real or have not and maybe never will happen. Many of us daydream about winning the Lottery for example! We can also express and understand abstract concepts such as love, truth and justice.

Our reasoning abilities are as impressive as our thinking abilities. We can work things out from basic principles and build up theories about how things work. Our intuition and deductive skills allow us to anticipate and make predictions about what is likely to happen in certain circumstances. We can also reason by analogy – using our experience in past situations to solve similar but new problems. Sometimes, our powers of thought allow us to make leaps of understanding that are Earth-shattering in their importance, as happened in the development of steam engines, the electric light bulb, the telephone and the computer. Most examples of our ability to think are more mundane, however, such as working out a cookery recipe from scratch, planning a touring route on holiday, or how to hit a billiard ball so it falls in a particular pocket. Although every-day thinking and reasoning are less impressive, they are still essential. A person who could not judge the speed of an oncoming car when crossing the road would not last long, however mundane the reasoning process!

The basic biological function underpinning all of our intellectual achievements is that of memory without which every new experience and item of information would have to be processed as if it was totally unique. The ability to register, store and retrieve information enables us to think about the past and imagine the future. We can manipulate stored information, reason about it and form new conclusions and ideas. This is what thinking is, and it is a skill that is better developed in humans than in any other species on Earth.

At six months Freddie will only remember things when they are placed in front of him

Deeds before thoughts

Babies are born knowing very little about the world they have just joined and unable to think in the adult sense of the word. From the moment of birth, however, babies start to learn about the world and build up the units of recognition that they need to help them acquire all the skills and knowledge they will need to function as independent human beings.

During the first few months of life, babies deal with the world mainly through actions rather than thoughts. A lot of physical development takes place – babies have to learn how to suck, lift their heads, reach out, sit upright and crawl – but during this time babies are also observing the people and items around them, interacting with them and noticing the effects of their own actions.

At first, babies are unaware of anything that they cannot immediately perceive – it is as if anything they cannot see or hear simply does not exist. Soon, however, they begin to recognise certain objects, even though they have no real conception of past, present or future. Baby Freddie, six months, likes to play with his baby gym, for example, and he is often given it. When his mother puts the gym in front of him, he will reach out to touch it, batting at the mirrors and coloured toys that hang from it, which helps him learn that it looks and feels a particular way. When he plays with the gym, Freddie has to remember how to put out his arm, how to shape his hand to grasp the toys and how to tap and rattle them. In these simple memories of his actions, Freddie is already creating the first building blocks of adult thinking. Without the ability to store experiences and objects in his memory, he would have to deal with everything as if for the first time. Even so, as a baby can only live in the present, Freddie needs to see the gym to think about it, and once it is taken away from him he probably won't remember it until the next time it is placed in front of him.

Babies seem to have an in-built ability to learn about and understand the physical world, however. They rapidly build up information gained by observing and interacting with their environment, and even young babies will look for explanations about why things happen. An infant will observe and learn about several different rules of physics just from sitting in his high-chair. Firstly, he will discover that solids can't go through solids – or, in other words, that his chair will support him and the tray in front will support his plate, spoon and rattle. Secondly, he learns that these items will remain stationary on the tray unless he pushes, pulls or picks them up – they will not move of their own accord. Thirdly, if he picks up the rattle and drops it over the side he learns that when things are let go they fall down to the ground and do not float upwards – an early illustration of gravity. He will also learn that if he makes a suitable noise, someone will come along to retrieve the item and give it back, so it can be dropped all over again. This lets him retest the observations he has made to see if the same physical rules apply next time round. He is already acting like a little scientist, like these babies:

Ellie, eight months, likes to push everything off her tray when she's in her high-chair. She really concentrates while she's doing it, then laughs with delight. She's trying to throw things off, too, now.

Although frustrating for the parent, messy eating provides an early lesson in physics for the child

> Jamie, nine months, turns things over and over in his hands, looking at them, and then does things like shake them, bang them together and bite on them.

By the age of eighteen months, infants have become experts at exploring their world. They now start to understand in their own minds how objects act in terms of physical movements and motions, and explore what objects will and will not do by trial and error and plenty of repetition.

This early understanding of objects allows young toddlers to reason by analogy – to work out how to solve a particular problem by thinking about a similar situation in which they successfully achieved what they wanted to do. For example, if a child has previously worked out how to insert a round-shaped object in a round hole, she may now reason that to insert a square-shaped object into the same educational toy she has to find a square-shaped hole. The quest for new information means that children of this age love taking things apart and trying to put them together again as part of the learning process. For example:

> Joss, eighteen months, likes taking everything apart. He likes to put objects back in boxes and help tidying up.

> Helena, two, thoroughly enjoys destroying the others' works of art! She will also get completely engrossed in building with bricks, etc.

Young children's explorations may even seem naughty at times, but really all they are doing is indulging the little scientist within as they try to make sense of various aspects of their world. They are also testing the rules they have developed about what is acceptable behaviour and what is not, for example:

> Natasha, twenty-one months, can be quite mischievous, for example, throwing crayons down the toilet, washing her trainers under the tap, drawing on the walls, throwing clothes into a bath full of water, etc.

Starting to think

As babies become toddlers, they show the first true signs of thinking as they become able to exercise their imaginations and start to use pretence. The things children learn about the world become consolidated through using the power of imagination in pretend play, but pretend play is about far more than just practising new skills. It is also one of the first clear steps that children take on the road to becoming thinkers. Children who can pretend can represent the world in an imaginary way in their own minds, and it is this skill that is the cornerstone of adult thinking.

Toddlers start to pretend at around eighteen months. Their pretence is very simple at first, but it is still a key step in developing their powers of abstract thought. Objects that children can see and play with usually act

Pretend play is one of the first signs of imaginary thought

as the catalyst for their first flights of imagination. Eighteen-month-old Freddie, for example, likes to play with a plastic tea set, and can imagine tea in the cup and food on the plate even though they don't exist. He happily pretends to drink tea and eat food, complete with sound effects! It's not a huge leap of the imagination, but for the first time he's thinking about something that isn't immediately in front of him, as are these children:

> The other day, Rosie, sixteen months, was playing with her little tea set when she poured herself a cup of tea and started pretending to drink it. She got really excited and was shouting, 'TEA, TEA, TEA!' and, I must admit, I was pretty excited too because I've never seen her pretend about anything before.

> Sam started to pretend around eighteen months, babbling into his toy telephone and pretending to eat plastic food. He also liked to cook invisible food in his toy saucepans.

As young children's ability to represent their world in their own minds develops, so does the complexity of their pretence. They gradually need less support from real objects and will soon pretend, for example, to drink a cup of tea without using a plastic cup as a prop – now they can imagine the cup as well as the tea. The next step is to take part in joint pretence, sharing a pretend game with another person. By two years of age, children are beginning to do this:

> Oliver, two, loves pretending with his father and me. His favourite pretend game at the moment is 'Sleeping Babies' – Daddy and I pretend to be babies sleeping, then we wake up and pretend to cry, until 'Mummy' Oliver finds a teddy or blanket to cheer us up saying, 'Don't cry, Baby, don't cry!' Oliver thinks this is hilarious. He also likes playing doctors, and we all take it in turns to have various imaginary injuries which get 'bandaged' up in his blankie.

As children build up memories of previous activities, they also start to talk about past and future events, but at this stage, although they are developing the ability to think in abstract terms, they usually rely on visual and auditory cues, such as photographs of where they have been or tunes that they recognise, to jog their memories.

> Thomas, two, saw a picture of his granny, and said, 'Granny. Granny, go to beach and sea.' His granny took him to the beach last time he saw her and I think he remembered when he saw her picture.

> We drove past a local restaurant today, and Oliver, two, pointed at it and said, 'Coffee there. Talk to man.' I was completely confused until I realised he was talking about going to the restaurant (about ten days ago!) where we ordered coffee from the waiter. I was surprised he remembered it because he hasn't mentioned it once in the meantime.

> Rianna, two, will sing whole nursery rhymes if she hears someone hum or sing the first line.

The world in symbols

As adults we represent our world using many different symbols. Using a symbol – something that stands for something else – allows us to share information, discuss and think about things that are not actually present. Our most important symbols are words and pictures. We use these to explain things to others and to understand what they in turn think about a subject. When one person says 'tree' to someone else, for example, they both know what that sound pattern (that is, word) stands for – the speaker doesn't need to produce the real thing. Imagine how difficult life would be if two people both had to be able to see or feel something simultaneously to talk about it – communication would be extremely difficult and talking about anything in the past would be completely impossible!

Children need to memorise and understand signs, symbols and language if they are going to take part in the world and make sense of it. Learning to use symbols like words and pictures helps them hold ideas in their imaginations and start thinking about things in an abstract way.

Recognition of speech sounds starts from before birth and continues afterwards when children are immersed in the spoken language of their carers. When children start to talk they learn to associate particular sounds with particular objects – they learn which sound symbols stand for which objects. This isn't always easy and young children often make mistakes when they first start to learn language. A common error is to call all round objects a ball, for example. In this case, a child may have worked out that the sound 'ball' is used to mean a round thing, but she does not know any other words for round things such as wheels, the sun or oranges. The best she can do with these objects is to call them balls. Similar common mistakes are to call all men 'daddy' or all animals 'dog':

> When Oliver was about eighteen months he saw sheep for the first time, but didn't know what to call them. He called them cows and doggies and cats one after the other, and looked very confused.

Adults tend to correct children when they use the wrong names for things. This feedback along with imitation, helps children to learn new words and work out more accurately what each word refers to. Humans have an inborn ability to learn language. Although learning how to talk is a huge task, children make rapid progress and by the time they have reached their sixth birthday, they will have learned an average of six to ten new words every day. Most young children also become involved in looking at picture books and focusing on the names of the objects, animals and people they see there:

> Ever since I can remember, Saxon has loved books and will pore over the pictures and words for long periods of time, learning the sounds and meanings they represent.

Looking at pictures and naming them helps children to come to grips with the most important symbolic system they will have to learn: the written words that depict their native language. 'Reading' with an adult helps children to understand that each word represents an object or concept and, eventually, that each letter stands for a sound.

Language is the most sophisticated tool we have for representing and recalling objects and events. Learning language enables children to describe their memories of an event to other people and share their experiences. As children's ability to remember things and think symbolically improves, so too does their grasp of language. By the age of three, children are generally able to describe things without having to see what they are talking about. For example, three-year-old Gabrielle went to the zoo and rushed up to her father to tell him about it when she returned home. She described the exciting animals she had seen, the cold reptile house and even her feelings about the animals. Although, at this

Looking at picture books will help eighteen-month-old Freddie
build his fledgling language skills

age, her recall is selective, and not particularly logical, she is able to tell her story without reference to visual cues – she no longer needs the lions and flamingos in front of her to remember and describe them and, with a little prompting from her father, is able to remember even more detail.

As they become even more adept with language and symbols, children may start to explore simple poetry, playing with the images and rhymes they can produce. For example:

> Georgie, four, loves playing with language and nonsense poems and will spend ages rhyming words. She came up with this with just the tiniest help from her dad . . .
>
> I despise
> fish eye pies.
> But frozen fish lips
> are delish lips.

Pictures, like written language, are symbolic representations of objects and ideas and, although drawing may seem like a purely recreational activity, it plays an important educational role. In fact, much of the information we gather is in the form of pictures as they can often help us understand complex concepts more easily than written words alone. Imagine trying to explain the exact layout of the planets in our solar system in an essay, for example, compared with how much easier this is using a diagram to show their relative orbits.

Children love to draw, but at the age of two just tend to scribble. They enjoy the movement of their hands and watching the trail of colour appear on the page more than making pictures themselves, and do not usually mind how their 'picture' turns out:

> Sam, twenty-two months, likes scribbling with coloured pens – he mostly draws lines and makes dots, or just scrawls all over the paper, which he often tears in his enthusiasm! Rianna, two, loves to paint. She paints over everything though, so the picture always ends up the same murky brown colour.

Between the ages of two and three, children start to realise that the marks they are making can represent things and they start to draw simple shapes like circles. Carmen, two, for example, drew a rough circle and said it was the sun. It might not look very like the sun to an adult, but Carmen clearly had an image in mind which she was trying to convey. From this very basic level of depicting an object, it is a small step to add eyes, mouth and legs to give the first hint of a human shape and features. Most children draw their first person at about three or four years of age. Carmen's sister Lana, three, drew a picture of Daddy, for example, shown as a circle with eyes, legs and hair. Lana is obviously more dextrous than Carmen, but she has also stored a more detailed representation of what her father looks like.

Trying to draw pictures of things, however badly, shows that children are capable of symbolic thought. They have built up an understanding of the world and formed mental images that can be communicated from memory using symbols. This ability is basic at first, but develops at a rapid rate. At this age, children also start expressing themselves using gestures as well as words. Some of these gestures will be copied from other people, but some may be made instinctively as children try to put their thoughts into words to express a particular meaning.

Thinking ahead

Symbolic thought is a vital part of being able to think and reason about the world in a logical way and allows children to start separating objects from the events with which they are involved. For example, children can now understand that a plate is an object in its own right, not simply part of the eating process. Similarly, symbolic thought enables children to separate their own thoughts and actions. They now realise that they do not have to be doing something in order to talk about it and can think, talk about and draw a picture of something from the past.

From the age of three, the way children's memories are retrieved and stored changes to become more efficient, so that new facts are easier to find and retain. They become able to think and reason about more complex concepts in a more advanced and logical way. They also become able to think and talk about past and future events without needing something to jog their memories:

> Alice, three, talks about her third birthday party (which was several months ago) and how much fun it was. She also plans for tomorrow – who she will see, what she will wear – when she will next go on holiday, when she will go horse riding again.

> Lana, three, is looking forward to Christmas this year, and knows what she wants and how Santa is going to get in to collect the cookies and milk she's leaving for him.

By four or five years of age they can recall events that have happened in the past in more detail and explain them to others. They can also plan ahead for particular events in the future in more detail than younger children. For example:

> Rebecca, four, likes to plan what she is wearing to a party and she has started to plan her list of friends and things she would like to do for her birthday party in January.

> Emily, five, plans for whether she will have five children or three – she thinks a lot about their names (at the moment the favourites are Sarah, Kate and Guido). She can't decide whether or not to marry (she's definitely not worried about whether anyone will ask her or not – she sees it as her decision alone). She talks a lot about whether it would be possible to live with her five children with me in the same house we live in now. She talks about whether I will become Granny Bridget or Great Granny when I am their respective ages, or whether I will still be Mummy Clare (she calls me 'Clare' and not 'Mummy' most of the time).

Finding out more

Children at this age also become incredibly curious about the world. They realise that the world is governed by certain rules, although they don't yet know what these rules are. They therefore strive to understand how the world works, so that it will become a more predictable and secure place in which to live. They do this by constantly asking questions and seeking answers. For example:

> Akira, four, is fascinated by numbers and he often asks me to count up to the last number. I never lie to him but I find it very hard to satisfy his enormous desire for knowledge. Lately he asked me, 'Mum who mounted the world?' And then, 'Who mounted people?', 'Who made London?', 'How many pieces does it take to make the world? Give me the number – 1000, 20000 . . . ?' One morning he opened the curtains to look outside and asked me what colour were the clouds. I said, 'Grey, they are grey!' He said, 'No, they are pink.' I said, 'Where can you see the pink? They are grey.' 'No,' he said. 'People are different and see things different . . .' Well what could I say?

As they try to find out more, four and five year olds spend increasing amounts of time exploring their world, experimenting, observing and discovering how the world works. For example:

> Rebecca, four, loves 'bugs' and in the summer she spends most of her time in the garden, looking at them through a special magnifying toy.

> Leon, four, watches his ice-cream melt, makes paper aeroplanes and flies them, sinks his boats and watches his egg timer.

> Suzanna, four, likes arranging things in a line or neatly in a box. She likes building towers and unpacking things!

> Tavey, four, likes digging in the sand-pit at the park. He has just started filling the lid of the sand-pit with water and putting all his toys and stones into it.

Charlie, four, understands the difference between spatial dimensions such as 'under', 'on top' and 'inside'

By four years of age, children have also acquired a greater spatial awareness, partly helped by their growing ability to draw what they see around them. If shown a scale model of a room in which a model item is placed while they watch, four year olds can work out logically where the real item is when entering the real room (with which they are familiar) featured in the model. This shows that children understand that the model is a representation or symbol of the room. They also have some idea of how different places link to one another topographically, although this understanding is still somewhat sketchy. For example:

I think Rebecca, four, understands that a journey links two places as we have family in Spain and Australia and we have travelled there.

Alex, four, is very conscious of how long it takes to get from A to B, even though he's not that sure how long ten minutes or half an hour is. He understands longer times like half a day or a whole day, for example to get to Scotland.

> Leon is only four, but he knows the route to school and can't stand deviation – he tells us we're wrong!

Four year olds are also increasingly familiar with the three dimensions of height, width and breadth, and can understand the meaning of spatial words such as inside, under and on top. These understandings tend to fall into place as their drawing skills become more advanced and help them develop a greater sense of space. Similarly, they learn to use words such as left, right and behind as their increasing linguistic skills help them to learn how to describe the relationship between different objects. For example:

> Georgie, four, drew five princesses and explained to me in great detail how, if you draw the girls with their clothes overlapping each other, that shows that one girl is standing behind the rest. She may look smaller, but she's not – she's just further away. Pretty impressive as a study in perspective, I thought!

Children can now draw things inside, under or on top of something else, and also experiment with these relative positions with their toys, water, sand and various containers:

> Rebecca, four, loves both water and sand. She will build sand-castles and dig holes in the sand. With water she loves splashing – filling up containers and pretending she's made a cup of tea.

> Leon, four, plays with water whenever he gets the chance. Runs taps, floats boats, fills jugs and jars, gets the mop and cleans the floors (leaving lots of water everywhere), gets a sponge and cleans the walls.

It's like this! Early reasoning

Preschool-aged children are able to represent their worlds in many ways – using words, pictures and their own imaginations for example – but they tend to see the world only from one point of view (their own!) and find it difficult to focus on more than one aspect of a situation or object at once.

For this reason concepts such as the appearance–reality distinction (the fact that an object can appear one way but be different in reality, as described in Chapter 3) are difficult for three to four year olds to grasp. Preschoolers tend to be influenced more by what they see than by what they know, and their reasoning is easily influenced by their own perception of the world (that is, appearance).

Even when they understand what the appearance–reality distinction is, young children will not always take it into account when thinking about things. For example, even though children are told that the Earth is round, most four year olds will still believe it is flat, as this is usually all they can see stretching in front of them – and in any case, if the world were round, wouldn't people on the bottom just fall off?

Akira, four, asked, 'The world is round? How do people stand upside down?'

Akira has reached this conclusion about the Earth by analogy from his everyday knowledge about balls and spheres. His comment shows that his knowledge of gravity and the universe has a long way to go, but it also shows that his analogical reasoning processes are developing well.

Reasoning by analogy is a basic but vitally important ability that we all use to solve problems. It enables us to use what we have learned from past experiences, by thinking about a situation where a similar problem was successfully solved on a previous occasion. This involves having a clear memory of the previous event and recognising that it falls into the same category as the current problem. Young children do not always find this easy as they are strongly influenced by the appearance of things, so do not always realise that two problems are similar in structure if they are about different topics.

Young children's tendency to focus on appearances rather than on logical reality can lead them to come up with some rather strange-sounding explanations of events. Their explanations are still based on what they see, rather than on what they can work out in their heads. For example, children aged around four often assume that the visible features of an object are related to what it does, for example, cows eat grass because it is green; dogs bark because they wag their tails; or bunny rabbits like carrots because they hop. For the same reason, children of this age tend to take everything very literally and may easily misunderstand things they hear or see. For example:

> The other day, Theo, five, said, 'Is Kishori normal?' Kishori is his little friend so I said, 'What do you mean?' and he said, 'Well, I want to phone her up and you always say "Normal people aren't awake yet".

Four and five year olds are still a long way from making sense of the world. They do not yet understand certain rules and still make judgements based on what they see. Their judgements are intuitive guesses rather than logical deductions about the world, although their ability to think in an abstract way is improving. Children do now realise that effects (for example, the ball moved) must have causes (for example, someone hit it with a bat) but they are not always accurate when working out what these are – they tend to associate events purely because they occurred in the same time frame.

For example, if a child falls off his bike and hurts himself as a result, he may correctly connect these two events in his mind but come up with the wrong causal explanation: 'I fell off my bike because I hurt myself.' Sadly, this can lead to children blaming themselves for catastrophic events within the family simply because the events have coincided with something memorable that they have done, for example, 'Daddy left home because I was naughty', or 'Granny died because I was cross with her for not giving me another sweet'. Because the two events happened around the same time, young children assume they must be related. The following is a good example of the associative reasoning that is typical of this stage:

> I was in the car with Fabian, five, and was turning the volume down on the stereo, when he asked, 'Mummy, how does the orchestra know to play more softly when you turn down the volume?'

Although children are not always accurate at generating correct explanations for themselves, they often do very well when given a situation and asked to choose the correct answer from a few given solutions. For example, if asked whether dogs bark because they are

149

excited, because their tails wag, because they gnaw bones or because they are brown, most four and five year olds would choose the correct causal response. Their emerging powers of deductive logical reasoning also mean that five year olds can usually work out the right answer if given two separate but related facts – even if the result is nonsensical. For example, if told that all cats are blue and that Joey is a cat, they will give the correct answer when asked if Joey is blue.

This suggests that their ability to think logically is starting to take shape. When asked to come up with explanations for themselves, however, young children's logic is still overwhelmed by what they can see. As such, they reason best about subjects with which they are very familiar. When they come across something new, they tend to rely on what they can see rather than on what they know.

Because they are easily influenced by what they see, four year olds also tend to assume that if an object's appearance changes then so does its reality. Just as they may think that when a girl puts on boy's clothes she actually turns into a boy, so they will also assume that other features of their world change according to their appearance.

For example, if a four-year-old child helps his brother count out two identical rows of coins, each of which contains ten pennies, he knows that each row contains the same number. If the coins in one row are then spaced out, however, so that the row appears longer, the four year old will say that the longer row contains more coins, even though he knows that none has been added. Similarly, if faced with two identical glasses of juice, one of which is then poured into a taller, thinner glass, a four year old will say that the taller glass now has more juice in it. In this task, known as a conservation task, four and five year olds have problems because they have seen something change and can only think about one aspect of the situation at once. They notice the longer row or taller glass, but fail also to consider the wider spaces or narrower width of the glass.

Although there is the same amount of juice in each container, four-year-old Abigail (below) thinks the taller glass contains more

Compare and contrast

By the age of six or seven, children start to understand that when a row of ten coins is spread out to look longer, it does not suddenly contain more coins. Likewise, they realise that the tall thin glass contains the same amount of milk as the shorter wider glass it was poured from. This is because children can now understand reversibility – that a change in appearance is reversible.

They can also think more logically and can hold more than one thing in mind. So in the case of the coins or milk, they now understand that if nothing has been subtracted or added then the amount must stay the same – even if it looks greater in some way. The ability to conserve quantity in this way helps children gain a new sense of stability and security – they now know that certain aspects of nature are permanent and unchanging, despite changes in outward appearance. Because they can now hold two aspects of a situation in mind, five to six year olds are better than younger children at comparing and contrasting things. This helps them start to understand and reason about quantities and relative amounts. They still do not fully understand distance, however. For example:

> The children know that a journey links two places and that you can go in a car, or train or aeroplane (even Aaron, two) but they have no concept of distance. Holly, seven, does, but Theo, five, might say, 'Does Yaya [Tooting, south London] live further than Uncle George [Brisbane, Australia]?'

> Emily, five, understands that a journey links two places but cannot understand about time and distance and place – she can't grasp that Cornwall is in England as opposed to being part of England, and our road is as big and real to her as the whole of London, which is separate to our road in her view.

Children's mathematical skills are advancing, however, and five to six year olds can understand the meaning of symbols such as +, = and − , can write numbers up to 100, and add and subtract numbers up to at least 10. Although they now understand that different coins have different values, and that different combinations of coins can add up to the same value, they still do not fully understand money or how much things cost. Even so, they now have a vested interest in looking after and saving their pocket money and some children are more aware of its importance than others:

> Jack, five, loves money and always has done since the age of two. He saves regularly and has more in the bank than me. He knows that you need money in order to buy things. He also knows that Daddy goes to work to make money for our house, food for us to eat, the car to drive, clothes to wear.

> Fabian, five, understands the concept of money but not the value yet I don't think, although he is very good at maths. He doesn't get pocket money yet, but if anyone gives him some money he carries it around with him for ages.

> Theo, five, thinks he can take us all out to dinner on twelve pence.

> Emily, five, is not as interested in money as Rory was at her age and doesn't notice if I forget to give her pocket money. She is very interested in numbers, but not particularly in money.

> Kishori, five, is starting to understand that money can get her things she wants and that different coins have different values. She does not yet save pocket money, although she keeps what she is given in a jar. She lets others have access to this jar, however, not appreciating its worth to herself.

> Ellie, five, does collect pocket money and has recently acquired a money box, but she doesn't understand how much things cost and not being able to afford things.

Children of this age can tell the time to the nearest half hour, and can also use simple comparisons such as bigger, smaller, less and more and understand how a pie can be divided up into different fractions such as ½, ¼ or ¾. These concepts are much easier for them to understand now that they can think about more than one thing and hold several ideas in mind simultaneously. Their interest in understanding the world continues apace too and is becoming more sophisticated, for example:

Nicola, six, often says she wants to do experiments. This usually means making a mess with various foods.

Theo, seven, has always liked DIY and is very good at fixing things. He really wants to know how mechanical objects work and will go to a lot of trouble to understand the process. He often knows how to fix his bicycle, can put stabiliser wheels on and off for his brothers, etc. He loved installing the irrigation system in our garden and was fascinated by how it works.

Rory, seven, is very much a little scientist by nature. He has a love of stones and rocks, is fascinated by insects and can be very gentle with, for example, spiders, letting them walk over his hand and inspecting them up close. On the beach he is totally absorbed for hours doing his own experiments with water, sand, stones, sea anemones, rock pools, etc.

Anmika, seven, looks out for magnetism and applies some of her school knowledge to every-day activities. She loves discovering things in the garden and plants seeds from fruit.

Georgie, seven, was explaining displacement to me in the bath the other day. 'Look Mum, if I go under the water, the waterline goes up.' He's a little mathematician and is very advanced for his age.

Nine-year-old Tsehai knows that she must cut the pizza exactly in half or Amalia will choose the larger piece

Learning mathematical principles helps children to realise that, as well as a brain, they have a memory and that repetition and practice will help to imprint facts more firmly in their minds. This understanding usually coincides with school tasks such as learning lists of words, spellings and numerical tables. Once they realise they have a memory, children will go on to rehearse things for themselves when they particularly want to remember certain facts such as the names and order of the planets in the solar system, or how to spell various dinosaur names. They now also start to gain a firmer understanding of the principles of cause and effect and to grasp more complex rules of physics.

> Fiona, seven, understands that to get the ball through the basketball hoop, she must throw it above the hoop as well as far enough (not straight *at* the hoop). She still can't do it though!

In theory

As children develop more efficient powers of memory and reasoning, and begin to understand more about how the world works, they start to generate their own explanations – or theories – about why things happen the way they do. When this first happens, around five or six years of age, children often become very caught up by reality.

Once they form a theory, five and six year olds will tend to apply it rigidly, even when faced with evidence to the contrary. When applying their knowledge or theories to a situation, they often show what psychologists call 'intellectual realism' and behave according to what they know intellectually rather than according to what they perceive. This can be easily illustrated by asking five or six year olds to draw a cup whose handle is pointing away, so it cannot be seen – they usually still draw in the handle even though it is not visible to them. They know that a cup should have a handle so they simply supply one.

Similarly, six year olds will draw the profile of a face in a Picasso-like way with two eyes rather than one. Although children can draw a facial outline accurately at this age, their knowledge that humans have two eyes overrides what they can actually see. Instead of using intuition and drawing what their eyes show them, six year olds switch entirely to logic and draw what they know is true – that human beings have two eyes. There is no room for exceptions to the rule and children are so involved with their knowledge that they completely ignore the visual side of a situation.

Although children know the difference between appearance and reality at this age, they still find it difficult to consider both at once, especially if the two seem to contradict each other, and now reality tends to hold sway over appearance. A simple yet interesting experiment to explore how children's thought processes affect their ability to solve problems involves the use of an unevenly weighted rod. Between the ages of three and four, children have no theories about how the world works but can use trial and error to make something happen. If a four year old is given a rod with a large, obvious weight on one end and asked to balance it on a rest, she will usually succeed at her first attempt. Although she knows nothing about fulcrums, pivots or equilibrium, she will balance the rod by trial and error, just moving it around until she finds the right balance point. A six year old will struggle with the same problem, however. He will typically try again and again to make the rod balance at its midpoint, pressing down furiously in his effort to balance it, without success. Eventually, when he continually fails to balance the rod, he will give up in frustration.

Why does a six year old find this problem so difficult when a four year old has no trouble? The answer is that the six year old has formed a theory about balancing things and, according to the rules he knows, the rod should balance in the middle. He is so convinced that his theory will work in practice, that he keeps trying to balance the rod at its middle point. He is relying rigidly on what he knows rather than using trial and error as a younger child does. Even if the six year old is shown a rod weighted in the same way as his, placed non-centrally on a fulcrum and balancing, he will probably refuse to copy this and change his theory.

Although the older child appears to have regressed because he can no longer balance a rod, he has not. He is now thinking in a more sophisticated and logical way. Building, testing and consolidating theories is a crucial part of children's development, and applying their rules rigidly is a stage that all children must go through in order to learn that the world does not operate in an all-or-none way. Once children realise this, they can apply their theories in a more flexible way and, by the age of eight, children can once more tackle the weighted-rod problem successfully.

Eight year olds will look at the rod, realise it is weighted at one end and guess the point at which it is most likely to balance. If they are slightly out, they quickly work out how to adjust the rod until they achieve the desired result. They now rely both on what they see and on what they know. They can accommodate exceptions to their rules and realise that they may need to apply a different approach if their initial attempts fail.

Eight year olds are also using more advanced reasoning when they balance the weighted rod. They can now think about more than one aspect of a given situation and, in this case, can take the weight of an object into account, as well as the relative position of its fulcrum. This is a big step forward in the thinking stakes as it involves holding two things in mind simultaneously, co-ordinating them and reaching a logical conclusion.

Abstract thought

From now on, children's ability to think abstract thoughts, form original ideas and make mental calculations becomes increasingly sophisticated – as does their personal experimentation. For example:

Majenta, eight, says she has tried flying and has tried breathing through a straw underwater in the bath.

Sophie, eight, experiments with freezing flowers in water. Her twin, Jamie often makes tools or toys out of twigs or bamboo canes, etc.

By seven to eight years of age, thinking abstractly also helps children to think clearly about their futures and to make much longer-term plans:

Holly, seven, hates throwing old toys and clothes away. She says, 'I want to keep them for my children.'

Rory, seven, plans for the future when he will have a bank account(!) and when he will go to a 'big boys' school'. He already asks about how you get money when you are old and have to stop working and was quite interested to hear about pensions! Like all kids he plans his Christmas present list and has already told me where he wants his birthday party in early April.

Max, seven, wants to get a job and earn some money when he is older (maybe after GCSEs). He says that if he marries a woman who also has a job they will have a good life.

Danielle, eight, plans for getting married and the kind of job she would like to do.

Children's ability to store and recall memories is also expanding, along with the development of memory-assisting strategies. This is illustrated, for example, when learning to play a piece of music. Children can now think of more than just the notes on the page and the correct position of their hands on the piano. To learn the piece sufficiently well to play without sheet music, they have to use their powers of memory and also devise internal strategies for remembering the order of notes. Because they are aware of their own memory and its limitations, children of this age start to break down the piece into manageable chunks – perfecting a few bars at a time. They will also be infusing the music with their own interpretation, style and expression to make the piece uniquely individual to themselves.

Seven and eight year olds can also tell the time to the nearest quarter of an hour and understand that matter can adopt different physical states (solid, liquid, gas) and can change from one state to another. They are now adept at using a ruler to measure an object's length and they understand certain principles of distance, such as the shortest point between A and B is a straight line joining them, and that if two routes are the same up to a point and then only one route continues, then that route is the longer one. Their understanding of distance is still imperfect, however, and if two runners run the same distance and one gets there before the other, seven to eight year olds may think the winner ran a shorter distance because they don't yet understand the relationships between speed, distance and time. Some will grasp the principles quicker than others as a result of their experiences. For example:

> Rory, seven, has always been keen on maps and interested in travel, particularly plane travel – he's been on long-haul flights and is always very good because he understands the concept of time and distance.

> Majenta, eight, understands that a journey links two places but doesn't understand distance.

Children now also have a greater understanding of the concept of money, as the following quotations show:

> Holly, seven, understands the concept of money. The children don't get pocket money, but Holly might say, 'When I've got some money I'm going to buy a make-up kit'. They are not very good at keeping money. When it's given to them they want to go out and spend it straight away. (I can't think where they get that one from!)

> Corey, seven, understands money. He gets one pound per week and occasionally saves up for a few weeks but he finds this hard and so spends his money and gets upset that his brother always has more than him.

> Theo, seven, is starting to understand the value of money. He puts his pocket money in a piggy bank, but sometimes if we're out and he has some money, he'll want to spend it just because he has it.

> Rory, seven, is a natural hoarder and collector and this extends to the stashes of money he has in his bedroom. He's saved fifty-one pounds from fifty-pence pocket money and money he's found over the last couple of years. He's already asking for a rise to a pound when he's eight. He is good at counting money and interested in how much things cost/relative values. He is interested in different currencies.

By the age of nine, children's ability to think logically and in abstract terms means that they can use decimal points, solve multi-step mathematical problems and understand the basics of geometry, which involves reasoning about space. They now realise that a short ruler and a long ruler will provide the same measurements for a room even though the shorter ruler has to be moved more often, and they also understand that length is unaffected by the direction of movement – so the drive from A to B covers the same distance as the drive from B to A along the same route. Children's knowledge of numbers and ability to think abstractly is now advanced enough to understand the principles of risk and chance:

Kaspar, nine, understands chance quite well and has a roulette game.

When I asked Christopher, ten, if he understood about chance, he replied, 'You mean probability?' He and Nicola, six, are fascinated by gambling! They wanted to teach poker to our next-door neighbour's girls (six) but we thought this was not a good idea.

Aisha, ten, understands that taking a chance can get you in trouble. She also understands that you could take a chance and do something you've never experienced, for example, bungy jumping.

Children can also think about the world in geological terms and can now understand how rivers, mountains and valleys are formed, as well as keenly continuing with their personal experiments:

Kaspar, nine, has done household experiments baking, growing cress and other things, and freezing water in a bottle. He tried to grow crystals and has a little electricity set which he loves.

Becky, nine, loves taking everything apart and putting it back together. We save broken appliances for her. She constantly acts like a little scientist – she mixes 'concoctions' to see how they turn out, makes paper aeroplanes and then tries tape, paper-clips, etc., to see what flies best.

Jonathan, nine, once put some limestone into a can of coke to see if it would dissolve.

Taliesin, nine, firmly believes he is a scientist and has his own laboratory space where he experiments in a scientific way and also in a fantasy way – this occurs on a daily basis.

The thinker

Around the age of eleven, children develop a deeper level of reflection about the nature of logic, theory and evidence which helps them think in still more complex and abstract ways about the world and the way it works. They can now hold five different facts in their short-term memory which helps them solve more complex problems, although they may not understand more advanced mathematical concepts until the ages of fourteen and fifteen, when they can hold around seven facts in short-term memory. Being able to keep multiple facts in mind enables them to keep intermediate results in mind and to progress a mental problem further, in order to come up with a solution.

Children are now able to reason out solutions to complex problems in an impressively adult way, however. They can come up with various hypothetical explanations for a problem and test these in a systematic and scientific manner. For example, if given a complex problem such as building a raft to cross a river, but only the basic materials needed to construct the raft, children of this age can generate several creative and sensible solutions, evaluate each suggestion, decide which to follow and carry out their chosen method of building a raft successfully. Their experimentation can also be surprisingly professional at this age:

Aisha, ten, likes to use scientific words when in the bath pretending her bath toys are instruments, i.e., saturated, insoluble, etc.

Thirteen year olds Imogen and Katie can now understand sophisticated concepts and solve complex problems

Billy, ten, is a real little scientist. He loves making potions, has an alchemy set, makes shampoo, weighs things comparing heavy and light, measures things – lengths in particular – and likes using magnets. He and Becky, seven, have collected insects from the garden and watched them through a spy glass. Billy, I am sad to say, pulled the legs off a daddy long legs to see if he would still walk with three legs.

Harry, eleven, loves to learn about why something works – so he'll read about something. Living next to the beach for three months, he was trying to understand all sorts of things about fishing, sea-urchins, natural rock salt, tides, etc. The *Guinness Book of World Records* is a favourite book of his. He loves astronomy.

Rowan, eleven, was recently interested in floating and sinking when he tried scuba diving. He has tried melting, burning, freeing various things. Aleishia, twelve, has experimented with gravity and floating.

During the next few years, children's power of thought continues to develop but even so, by eleven, a child can already hold several things in mind simultaneously, make comparisons, plan ahead, reason hypothetically and form increasingly complex theories. The child who once understood the world only in terms of action has now developed into an adult – a true thinker – who is capable of thinking in a number of advanced, original and flexible ways. Just how far this ability will take each individual in terms of career, inventing new technologies and solving previously insoluble problems depends on his or her intelligence, knowledge and memory, and how these skills are used. With a little tuition, however, the majority of adults have enough thinking power to cope with most of life's challenges – even road works, multiple routes and diversions!

It is a long journey for a child to become a fully thinking adult

chapter five

life and times

|ife and time are intricately related for most of us. At the level of every-
day activities, we follow various daily routines and we structure our
days around the regular and essential activities of eating and sleeping.
As adults, many of us also organise our days around other important
deadlines such as school-runs, work and prearranged meetings with
friends or colleagues. We measure time in many ways – minutes, hours,
days, weeks, months, seasons, years – and live our lives accordingly. We
plan ahead, take photographs to remind us of times past, keep diaries
and use calendars. Time is so much a part of our every-day lives that
many adults would feel lost without a watch or clock nearby!

At a much broader level, however, adults also understand that life
itself runs a particular course and changes over time. We recognise that
the world is divided into two types of entity: those that are living and
those that are not. We also appreciate that living things have special
qualities which allow them to evolve and reproduce their own kind before
they grow old and die. In humans, this life cycle is maintained by our
instinctive drives towards eating, drinking, sleeping and having sex, all
of which are vital for the continuation of our species.

In fact, our life cycle is the basis for most human activities. For our
children to grow and ourselves to survive we must provide nutrition by
tending crops, buying groceries, planning meals and learning how to
cook. To attract a mate we select flattering clothes, follow the grooming
rituals of our gender and socialise to interact with the opposite sex.

Humans are dominated by their basic need to reproduce

Reproduction is the only biological feature of our life cycle over which we have any control – science having successfully uncoupled reproduction from our recreational need to make love. The ability to plan whether or not we have children, how many and when, is one of the most significant steps we have taken as a species, for the drive to reproduce is so strong that we are in danger of overpopulating our planet. At the other end of our life cycle, adults also know that we will all die someday – in fact, this is the only event that we can be absolutely certain will occur at some stage in our future as we follow the path from cradle to grave.

Despite the fact that they are an intrinsic part of the human life cycle, babies are born with no knowledge of it. They have strong drives to feed, sleep and seek company and stimulation, but babies have no conception of the difference between living and non-living things and no awareness that, even though they are now alive, the progress of life and time means that one day they will inevitably die. Similarly, until puberty kicks in and their sex hormone levels rise, the only interest children have in the opposite sex is as playmates rather than partners.

Much of what children learn about the human life cycle, particularly about sex and death, depends on what their parents tell them, although they will also pick up information from their peers (not always accurate!), television, biology teachers, newspapers, books, magazines and – increasingly – the Internet. Children may recite certain facts at different ages, but they will not fully understand abstract concepts such as life and death until they have the mental capacity to do so. By the time they reach independence, however, children need to have grasped the fundamental difference between living and inanimate objects, learned the ins and outs of the facts of life and accept the knowledge of their own mortality.

Early awareness of life

Although scientists are confused about the exact nature of what constitutes 'life', even young children seem to be aware that living beings have some hidden, internal essence which makes them special in a certain way.

Newborn babies seem to have an in-built sensitivity towards other human beings. At birth, babies can only focus clearly on objects within about 25cm of their faces. Nonetheless, they show a distinct interest in human faces and tend to look at a human face longer than anything else in their environments. Babies are also fascinated by moving objects and, by only three months of age, they can differentiate between movement that is biological – like the movement of people or animals – and movement that is mechanical in nature. By about nine months of age, infants even show a distinct preference for biological movement.

Newborns are particularly attracted to human faces

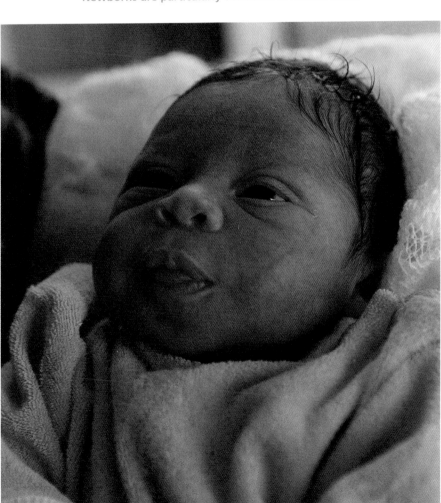

The difference between living and non-living things is one of the first and most important conceptual distinctions infants make. From around the age of ten months, infants become capable of grouping many of the objects they observe in the world around them into categories. By the age of one, infants can recognise objects (including living things) as belonging to distinct groups and can categorise living species remarkably accurately, based on their external appearance. They have observed that a dog is different from a table or a flower, or even a cat, for example.

As they continue to observe the world around them, children's ability to categorise objects into broadly similar groups helps them to recognise certain differences between things that move and are alive and things that move but are non-living – although infants obviously have no understanding of what these differences signify. By the age of twelve to eighteen months, toddlers given a toy bird and a model plane to play with will make them move in distinctly different ways even though they look very similar. A child may, for example, make the toy bird hop along the ground while the model plane is made to glide along the ground or through the air. But, even though children of this age have made a distinction between the movement of biological and mechanical things, they don't yet understand that one is living and one is not. They just recognise that the two things are quite different in some basic, fundamental way.

By the age of two-and-a-half, children have started to recognise the finer distinctions between different species and, even though they have never seen one, will class a triceratops with a brontosaurus rather than with a rhinoceros, for example, despite obvious surface similarities between the two. To make these distinctions, children seem to focus on several basic features such as position of ears, thickness of legs, body proportions and the shape of head or tail, as well as the way animals move and behave. Children of this age can also make finer distinctions within a species, such as telling different types of dog or cat apart from each other.

Children love learning about animals, especially those that are small, furry, friendly and cuddly, although when encountering anything new,

Sarah, eighteen months, knows that biological and mechanical things move in different ways

they will remain naturally wary until they are reassured that the animal is harmless. Children have the opportunity to learn about animals from many different sources: through close contact with family pets, watching animal programmes on TV or video, looking at animal picture books and by visiting theme parks, zoos and farms:

Maxim, two, is mad about animals. He asks me to take the rabbit out of her cage so that we can brush and stroke her, he covers her in kisses and wants to hold her. He's desperate to meet dogs, cats, etc., and talks about the horses, sheep and cows we've seen in the country.

Oliver, two, has loved animals from a very early age. His favourite books have always been animal ones, even when he was less than a year old.

Observing animals helps children to gain some understanding of the differences between things that are living and things that are not, although at this stage their understanding is fairly sketchy and mainly based on whether or not things can move:

> Aaron, two, sometimes knows what things are living and what aren't. He might say about a toy, 'It can't talk, silly, it's a teddy.'

> Maxim, two, has a problem with telling the difference between things that are living and things that are not. He is afraid of lots of inanimate objects because he thinks they are alive. The other day he asked me for a wooden Pinocchio toy, but then while I was changing his nappy he got very worried and said, 'Pinocchio bite my willy.'

Interacting with animals can also give young children a gentle introduction to the realities of life and death as the following quotation suggests:

> Louie, two, loves animals and did have two rabbits living on the balcony, but a fox killed them.

Living in the present

Learning about animals also helps children grasp another important concept – that of growth – as they start to realise, for example, that a puppy is not only a type of dog but a baby dog that will grow up to be an adult dog. At the age of two, however, toddlers live firmly in the present and have no idea that they were once babies, or that babies grow to become bigger children and then adults. Toddlers assume that everyone – including themselves – has always existed in their current form and always will:

> Tré, twenty-two months, does not realise he was once a baby. He still is to me, but he thinks he is a big boy.

As a result of this assumption, toddlers will assume they are looking at a picture of another baby they currently know when shown pictures of themselves as babies:

> Aoife, two, doesn't recognise herself as a baby in photos. In photos of when she was about one year old, she knows it is her but says things like, 'Where's my hair?' because it was a lot shorter.

> Oliver, two, will tell us that a picture of him as a baby is 'a baby', or 'Baby Toby' (a friend's baby). Sometimes he'll say it is 'Baby Oliver', but if we say, 'Is that you?' he always says, 'No, it's Baby Oliver.'

Similarly, when toddlers see family videos they can recognise their mothers and fathers, who usually look much the same as they currently do. But when they see themselves as infants, young children are often convinced that they are looking at a baby brother or sister. They do not yet know that living things change and grow. This is partly because children of this age base their reasoning purely on what they can see, and since growth takes place over a period of time it is not an immediately observable event.

Understanding time

Young children also find reasoning about past and future events difficult, as discussed in Chapter 4. Two year olds are only just developing the ability to think in abstract ways and their memory is limited. This makes it difficult for them to grasp the concept of time and, without a sense of time, it is hard to understand the concept of growth. As a result, they do not understand that babies (or, indeed, they themselves) will grow into adults in the future or that their mother was once a little girl.

Lacking an accurate conception of time also means that young children do not grasp the meaning of age. Children of two and three can often say how old they are and hold up the right number of fingers when asked, but this simply reflects the fact that they are good at learning their own labels, such as their name and gender. At this stage, they do not actually understand what these numbers represent and often believe that someone's age is related only to their size, so that bigger people are automatically regarded as older even if they are the same age or even younger, as the following example shows:

> Just before his birthday, Saxon, now four, announced that Nathan was older than him 'because he is taller'.

In young children's minds, Granny was born a long time ago and dinosaurs lived a long time ago – so they will happily assume that Granny and the dinosaurs co-existed. After all, they cannot comprehend how long just one year lasts, let alone millennia!

Children's grasp of time starts to develop not through learning about hours and minutes, clocks and calendars, but through becoming familiar with what happens along the timeline of their own daily routines. They learn that, after waking up, they get dressed and then have breakfast, and that after tea there is bath time, followed by a bedtime story before snuggling down to sleep. It is these familiar patterns that define how a day passes for young children. Hence a two year old who falls asleep in the afternoon, when he usually only sleeps at night, may wake up and think it is already the following morning:

> Thomas, two, rarely sleeps in the day now. The other day he did have a nap, and when he woke up he expected to have breakfast and asked for cereal!

Although children at this age recognise the patterns of their daily routines, their understanding of time is still very basic. They can recognise the difference between past and future very broadly, and will begin to talk about past events occasionally, but they cannot understand more sophisticated concepts. At this stage, children can only recognise whether something is happening 'now' or 'not now'. Statements such as 'later', 'in five minutes', 'tomorrow' or even 'next year' do not have any firm meaning and all just signify 'not now':

Jashan, two, uses soon/later and is starting to grasp the meaning i.e., later = not now. He still mixes up before/after but understands that they are different concepts. He also uses yesterday/tomorrow but uses the words interchangeably and randomly so that we have to work out what he means by the context. He cannot yet understand last week/next year.

Aaron, two, knows that 'soon' and 'later' mean 'not now'. He might say, 'I don't want to go to nursery' so I say, 'We're not going now, we're going later.' Then he's happy even if later means in ten minutes. He often says, 'Is it the middle of the night?'

Two-year-old Helena's concept of time is still quite limited and, as such, although she understands words like 'last week' and 'next year', she does not necessarily understand what next year is (if you know what I mean).

Not understanding time means that young children often seem incredibly impatient and will keep interrupting your conversation if they want to gain your attention. Two and three year olds have no idea what phrases such as 'wait a minute' mean as they have little or no recollection of past events where 'waiting a minute' produced a satisfactory result. They need to say what they want to say now, straightaway, while the impulse is still there, otherwise their minds will move on to a new set of thoughts and they will forget what they wanted to share. Having to last even a minute without doing what they want to do seems an interminable length of time to two and three year olds. As a result, the pleasure of gaining your attention becomes completely lost in the frustration they experience when they cannot have you all to themselves at that very moment. Their self-centred view of the world also contributes to this urge, as they do not understand that other things may hold your attention.

Maxim, two, will ask again and again for something he wants. If we're in the car and he wants his juice, he'll shout and shout at me until I can stop and get it for him.

Helena, two, will wait for something that she needs, but is something of an old nag, going on and on until I'm worn down and get her what she wants.

Rebekah, three, cannot really wait for something she needs, though she's improving. She can still jump up and down in temper if not handed the sweet quickly enough or start shrieking if someone else gets it before her.

By the age of three, children's memories are improving and they have a firmer feel for time, although it is still based on what they experience during a typical day, or reflects what they have been told. Children can now use simple time-linked words such as 'when' and 'last night', but generally do so only in relation to known and repeated events (for example, when I have breakfast, I eat porridge); they still cannot use these terms in an abstract way. If asked when nursery school ends, for example, three year olds will not say, 'At half past three' or 'In two hours' time', but will typically answer, 'When Mummy comes to pick me up.' These children are beginning to use time-linked words in generally appropriate ways for example, but still do not understand the exact meaning of various abstract words that are used to define particular points in time:

Lana, three, refers to every past event or experience as happening 'yesterday'.

Euan, three, has started understanding yesterday/tomorrow, but has problems with last week/next year.

Rosa, three, uses 'Not the next day, but the next day' to clarify future dates. She also uses 'next week' for last week or yesterday.

Ewan, three, understands before and after, for example, 'No milk before lunch' or 'You can have a sweetie after you've eaten all your dinner'.

Two-year-old Tré wants to go on the swings now; he is too young to understand the concept of 'later'

As children of this age do not really comprehend time, they may also have difficulty understanding the need to hurry when asked. Three-year-old Alice, for example, knows that after breakfast she is allowed to play and that after playtime she will leave for nursery. However, she puts everything that has already happened under 'past' and everything that has not yet happened under 'future'. Whether she is leaving for nursery in five minutes, five hours or five days makes no difference at all to her . . . it all comes under the same heading of 'later'. As a result, in Alice's mind, there is no such thing as 'late', so, much to her mother's exasperation, she will continue playing with her dolls when asked by her mother to hurry. Hurrying makes little sense to Alice at three years of age.

Around the age of four children's ability to grasp abstract concepts improves noticeably. They become able to think about more than one thing at once and now start to realise that 'yesterday' and 'tomorrow' are relative terms, making sense only in comparison to 'today'. As children grapple with these ideas, their understanding of time starts to become more advanced and they learn to relate time to their every-day experiences:

My youngest asked me, when he was four, 'Is it yesterday today, or is it tomorrow?' When I answered that it was today, today, and that it is always today, today, he told me that that was impossible . . .

Akira, four, knows the day by breakfasts – each day is one breakfast so, for example, his dad may come back in seven breakfasts.

Alex, four, understands yesterday/tomorrow – he works it out in sleeps. Tomorrow is after this sleep.

Four year olds still have difficulty in thinking about time as being separate from activities, however. They may assume that time passes quickly when they are having fun, drags slowly when they are waiting for something, and that clocks and watches stop when they are asleep because they do not directly experience this time as it passes. Because time is not thought of as separate from activities, it can be even more difficult to persuade a child of four to hurry up, even when they are told they will be late – there are so many distractions filling their minds with interesting and wonderful thoughts that hurrying almost seems like a waste of time.

> Rebecca, four, will try to hurry up but it doesn't seem that fast to me. She seems to be on 'slow' when you are in a particular hurry.

> When we are in a hurry, Saxon, four, has two speeds: 'dead slow' and 'stop'.

> Akira, four, doesn't hurry when we are late for school. For him, it is not that bad to be late, so we are always late at school. Just once he said he didn't like to be always late, but he didn't change his attitude.

> Tavey, four, won't hurry unless I say that he'll miss something, but even then not much. The best way to hurry him is to say I'm going without him.

Instant gratification!

Children's concept of time can be illustrated with a simple experiment, which involves offering them two pieces of chocolate, one being a single square, the other being a whole bar. They are told that they can either have the single piece now or they can have the whole bar in ten minutes' time, if they wait.

Children who live in the present and do not understand time will want to eat the single square of chocolate now. Their thoughts are overwhelmed by what they can see and smell, and ten minutes later just means 'not now' to them – it could even mean next year. To children of two, who are at this stage of development, the choice they have been offered is essentially a choice between having some chocolate now or not now, so any self-respecting two-year-old chocolate lover will thus choose the 'now' option in no uncertain terms. For example:

> Jashan, two, would want one square now (*and later!*).

> Dominic, two, would want a piece of chocolate NOW.

Three year olds, who only have a limited notion of time, will also tend to want one square now rather than a whole bar in ten minutes' time:

Trimane, three, said he would like the little piece of chocolate now.

Rebekah, three, would choose the chocolate now, please.

Abigail, three, would choose the piece of chocolate now, but would have a tantrum and demand the whole bar now as well.

By four years of age, children are beginning to understand the basics of time. They will probably want the whole piece now, but may have enough understanding to reply, 'The whole bar later.' Waiting for ten minutes is difficult for four year olds, however, and they may want to put the chocolate somewhere else, or hide their eyes, so that they cannot see it while they wait. If they can see the chocolate, four year olds often find it especially difficult to wait as what they can see in the here and now will still tend to overpower their logical reasoning (which tells them that waiting for a whole bar is the best option). Those who do choose to wait may also attempt to distract themselves while waiting by singing, counting or repeating a nursery rhyme. Four year olds can thus give very different answers in this experiment, all of which are perfectly normal at this age:

Leon, four, would want one piece of chocolate NOW NOW NOW.

Tavey, four, would probably demand all the chocolate now and refuse to accept the choices.

Reece, four, would choose a whole bar in ten minutes, but would ask every minute if the ten minutes were up.

Katie, four, waited for the whole bar, and sang the alphabet song continually until the ten minutes were up.

The chocolate experiment, clockwise from top left: Aoife, Gabrielle, Alex and Ewan are put to the test

Rebecca, four, loves chocolate but has the will-power to wait and have the whole bar. She will try and negotiate with you on how soon she can have it.

Jake, four, would probably wait for the whole bar.

By the age of five, children are developing stronger reasoning abilities and have a better understanding of time. They now understand that they can have more chocolate in ten minutes' time, and that ten minutes is not too far away. So five year olds will usually choose 'the whole bar later' and wait (sometimes patiently!) to receive their reward:

Jack, five, is very good at waiting for things. He would choose a whole bar in ten minutes.

Emily, five, would choose the whole chocolate bar in ten minutes.

Dead or alive?

By the age of three, most children have learned enough about growth and the passage of time to realise that, although they are not a baby now, they were once very small:

Jashan, who is almost three, knows he used to be a baby and objects to being treated like one now!

Rebekah, three, is beginning to understand she was once a baby, but generally thinks every photo of her as a baby is her new sister, Zoe.

Between the ages of three and four, as they start to understand the concepts of time and growth, children also start to be able to make the distinction between what is living and what is not. At this age, children make their decisions about whether or not something is living based

Emily, five, knows it's best to wait for the whole bar – though that doesn't make the wait any easier

largely on observable characteristics such as whether it moves, breathes and eats. For some items, this method leads to a clear and easy decision, but for other things the answer may not be so obvious. For example, children of this age can generally decide correctly that goldfish and rats are alive, while cameras and rocks are not. They may experience far more confusion with things like plants, dolls or talking robots, however. These things don't move, or they look like people, or they appear to talk and move but not eat . . . so are they living or not?

Given a goldfish, rat, plant, rock, camera, doll, maggots and a robot-dog, Ewan and Euan, both three, put everything in the 'living' category. Sicily and Francesca, both four, kept changing their minds and everything went in both categories at some point. Leon, four, got everything right except the plant, while four year olds Cory and Reece decided that maggots were not living.

As this example illustrates, three year olds tend to assume that dolls and robots are living things. By four years of age, children generally decide correctly that these objects are not living, but they may still show some confusion. But the fact that they are not sure shows that children of this age are starting to become aware that there is more to life than meets the eye.

Young children's uncertainty about what is living and what is not also shows in their tendency towards animism – that is, their inclination to treat many objects, especially toys, as if they are alive. 'Teddy can't see!' a child may cry if her parent walks in front of Teddy and obscures his 'view' of a favourite video. Teddy might also have to be 'fed' at meal times and 'need' stories read to him before bed. Likewise, a table or chair may receive a telling-off for 'bumping into' a youngster! Animism may be partly a reflection of young children's assumption that everyone and everything in the world experiences it in the same way that they themselves do. However, it is also likely to reflect an incomplete understanding of the nature of many objects and uncertainty about what 'life' actually is.

Cory, Sicily, Francesca and Reece are tested to see whether they can tell the difference between 'living' and 'non-living' things

Children's understanding of growth is also limited at preschool age. Preschoolers may think that a seeded crystal is alive because they can watch it 'grow' or that a spinning top is living because when it moves it may look as if it gets bigger. Similarly, they will still be confused about whether a slow-growing plant is really alive – it does not move and they cannot see it breathing. Interestingly, young children do seem to realise that plants are different from both animals and man-made objects, which suggests that they think of plants and animals as belonging to different biological categories, even though both are living things.

Children are now starting to realise, from their own experience of being alive, that living things have special characteristics. Four to five year olds can say that something which is alive can breathe (as they themselves do), heal itself (sometimes with the help of a plaster!), needs food and water (when hungry or thirsty) and has a mother – although as baby animals such as puppies, kittens, calves and lambs are often seen with only their mothers, young children do not always realise that living things also have fathers.

The birds and the bees

An intrinsic part of being alive is the ability to reproduce. Young children may realise that they might have children themselves one day, but they generally have little idea of the mechanism by which this will happen. Children's understanding of sex and reproduction largely depends on how much they are told by their parents, and hospitals or 'Mummy's tummy' may figure large in their minds. Even if children can recite that a baby comes from Mummy's egg and Daddy's sperm, they still have no idea what this means – these are just words they have been told and can remember.

Although young children are unlikely to understand the way reproduction works until they are older, they can understand that animals pass on certain traits to their offspring, such as hair and eye colour. Even though biological inheritance is quite a complex concept, at a basic level it does fall within young children's realm of personal experience. They also realise that, like a baby cuckoo, an animal that is reared by a different family will still have the characteristics of its biological parents. Some three to four year olds even realise that certain things such as running speed are not just inherited but can be improved by practice or training.

By the age of four, children have started to understand the difference between males and females. Comparing and exploring their genitals is a very important step towards finally realising the difference between males and females and learning about biological sex. As mentioned in Chapter 3, the following quotations are typical of this age:

> Nicola had a boyfriend during the preschool time and once they tried to look at each other's differences.

> Jake, four, is very penis aware, retracts his foreskin in the bath and is proud of his erection.

By the time they are four years old, most children know that they were once babies, that they came from Mummy's tummy and perhaps something along the lines of Daddy puts a seed into Mummy's tummy which grows into a baby. This is not real knowledge, however; these are simply statements that children have heard and remembered. Up to the age of five, children have no real understanding of birth or sex and are unable to think about the complexities of the human life cycle or the meaning of death. They cannot yet conceive of something that exists as not existing and may ask where they were before they were in Mummy's tummy.

Although four year olds are starting to understand that it is only girls who will grow up to be women and have babies, the details are very sketchy in their minds. The following quotations are wonderful examples of four year olds' thinking about this subject:

> Suzanna, four, thinks babies come from Mummy's tummy – out of the tummy button.

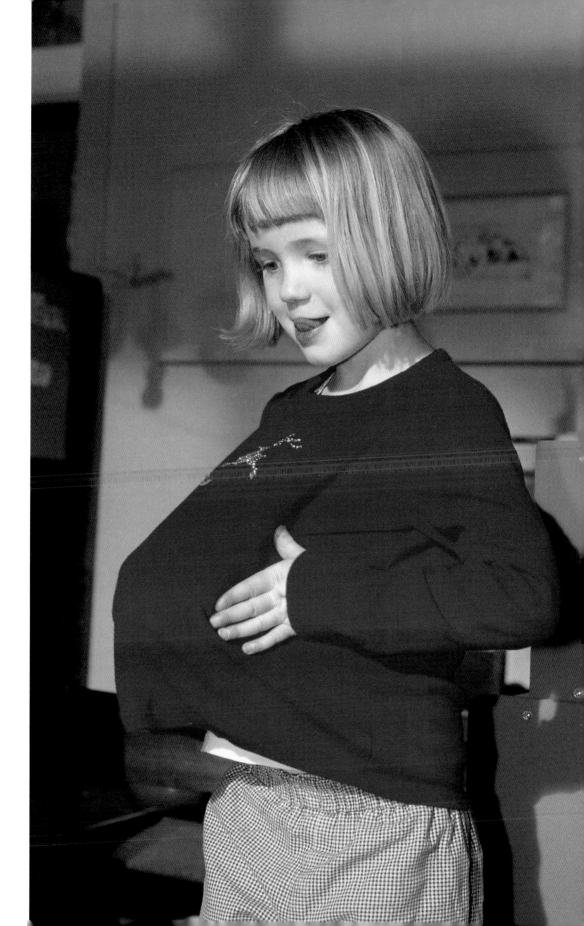

Bradley, four, thinks that babies come from where Mummy's wee comes from.

Alex, four, knows that babies come from Mummy's tummy and before that they were a twinkle in Mummy's eye, for example, in the wedding photos, when Alex asks where he was!

Rebecca, four, doesn't understand a lot about sex – I hope. Like most children, her naïvety and innocence is lovely and the things she says at times do make me laugh or cringe with embarrassment. One time in a restaurant (her voice can be quite loud) she asked if she came out of my tummy. I thought honesty would be the best policy so I said that she grew and developed in my tummy, but came out of 'Mummy's minny' to which she replied, 'Oh my God, Mummy, you must have a really big hole', much to the amusement of all sitting around us.

Four year olds do not really understand adult relationships either, but many will say they have a 'girlfriend' or 'boyfriend' as they start to gain a greater sense of independence and spend more time with their peers:

Apparently Jake, four, has a girlfriend, Cheyenne, his own age. Cleo (who is two) is apparently too young, as he needs a more mature woman at his age.

Georgie, four, has no real boyfriends yet, but does tell me how she's going to marry Lawren or Chad (she's really into weddings!).

Saxon, four, wanted to take a ring to school so he could marry Phoebe. Then, he said, they would be able to do a 'married kiss' like he'd seen on television.

At four, children may hold hands, cuddle and even kiss each other, but the idea of adults doing the same thing is usually met with peals of laughter or curiosity at this age of true innocence:

Suzanna, age four, shows us where babies come from

Rebecca, four, once saw a man kissing some girl on TV and saw a little bit of tongue which she thought was absolutely hilarious and also a disgusting thing to do.

Georgie, four, understands nothing about sex other than that there are males and females. If she sees a love scene on TV she is quizzical – 'What are they doing? Are they going to get married?'

Saxon, four, saw a passionate kiss in a film late one night and said, quite matter-of-factly, 'Oh look. They're doing a married kiss. Children aren't allowed to do married kisses like that until they're married, are they?'

The end of days

Children under five have a very limited understanding of death, as well as life. The concept of death is understood only in a cartoon way – Tom and Jerry invariably bounce back from the brink, but never actually disappear – and, at this stage of their development, children do not realise that a person or animal who is dead will never come back to life. Instead, they see death as a temporary state, like sleep, and usually think of a dead person as existing somewhere else, such as in heaven or even under the ground. The quotations capture three year olds' notions of death:

Alice, three, understands about a worm or fly or snail dying and she loves killing them. She understands that cartoon characters can be killed. I don't think she has any concept of a human being dying or being killed in real life. She does try to put flowers she has broken off at the stem into the earth thinking they will go on living.

Trimane, three, thinks that if you die you go to hospital. He doesn't understand death.

Children often pretend to be ill or dead, but at this age they don't understand what that means in real life

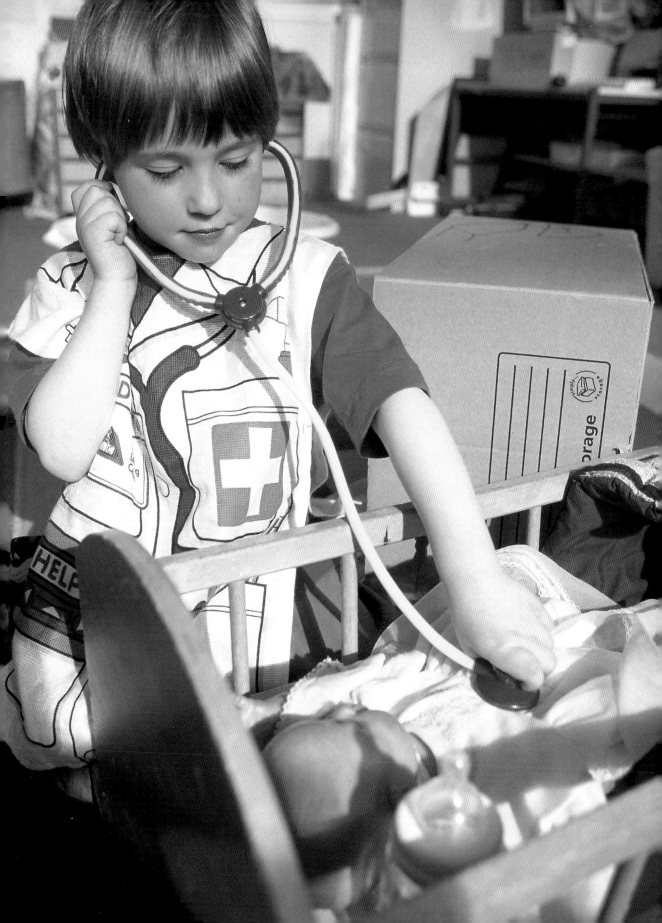

Sammy, three, only understands a little about death. He still thinks they will be alive again after.

Alex, five, said the goldfish that died (because Ewan overfed it) had gone to 'fish heaven'. Ewan, three, still insists it went to London.

Contact with animals is one of the commonest ways in which children are introduced to the concept of death, which they have to learn to differentiate from other non-moving states such as sleep. Children at this stage think of death as something that will not affect them personally and often confuse it with sleep. It is also common to think that someone or something dead has just gone away, as the goldfish to London quoted above illustrates.

By the age of four or five, many children will appreciate that someone who is dead will not come back, but it may not upset them unduly if they do not see it as personally relevant. For example:

When Saxon, four, was watching a programme about dinosaur bones, he asked, 'Mummy, when I die will I become a skull?' The next evening, he watched a programme in which a baby lynx died and, as the zoologist collected its body, he said, 'Look, the lynx is going up to heaven in a plastic bag.'

Akira, four, understands about death. He went through a stage when he was always asking about it. One day he came up to me and said, 'Mum, when someone dies it means that his story is finished!' I loved that and said, 'Yes, that's right.'

Although some children are not scared at the thought of death, it may start to upset or worry other children who are just beginning to grasp the concept:

Saxon, four, sometimes holds my face and looks troubled while saying he doesn't want me to die. Recently, he asked his granny whether the fact that she had grey hair meant she was going to die soon.

Trimaine and Reece try to wake up a dead hare

Alex, four, knows that when you die you don't wake up again but become an angel who goes up to heaven to be with God and Jesus. He is not frightened by the concept of death as he wants to be an angel and fly! However, he is scared that he could be knocked down by a car and never wake up.

Rebecca was two years old when my father died and because we are a very close family she was very upset. I have said he is in Heaven and he is happy, but still today (she is now four) she says she misses him and will cry about not being able to see him. She is frightened of her family dying. She has a great granddad in Australia who is 100 years old next year and Rebecca says will he die when he is 101 – to which I say you can never know when someone will die.

Once children can understand time, they can understand that people and animals may change as they grow and develop and realise that we all follow a life cycle, which includes birth, growth, the opportunity to reproduce and death. Although children now realise that death is final, and that people or animals who have died will never come back, they will not yet understand the full implications of this. Their beliefs about what happens after death will depend on what they are told and the religion or culture in which they are reared.

I think Fabian, five, understands that death is final. We talk about the fact that we will all die one day, and both Theo, seven, and Fabian are aware of this but quite comfortable with the thought that it won't happen for a long time.

His grandmother passed away last year whom Jack, five, knew well. He knew that she was sick and that she is now in a place where she is happy and well. He asks about his grandfather who passed away before he was born. Jack is very interested and curious. He really wants to understand what it is all about.

Nicola, six, understands that one day she will die, and that it means 'I will not see the world any more'.

When asked about death, Kishori, five, says, 'You can't hear and you can't talk. You can't open your eyes and you can't walk. You can't come back to your home for ever. You can come back if you get a new life like into an octopus.'

The life cycle

As children grow older and reach school age they become able to understand more complex concepts and so can appreciate family relationships and the dynamics of various life cycles. Up until this stage, children have based their knowledge solely on what they can see. To younger children, for example, Granny is a granny because she has white or grey hair. Three year olds do not understand that Granny is also the mother of one of their own parents.

Alice, three, calls old ladies 'grannies'.

I don't think Trimane, three, understands his grandparents are older than me.

Children's grasp of the fact that their grandparents are older than their parents depends upon their understanding of time, which they are now starting to develop. For example:

Georgie, four, understands that her grandparents are older than us and reminds us to go slowly when out with her grandma as she can't walk so fast.

Alex, four, is very conscious that his grandparents are older and that 'Gran is Daddy's Mother'. He seems to understand the whole set-up.

About a year ago, I discovered that Fabian was under the impression that the son of a friend of my mother's was her husband. Until recently (he is now five) he used to ask lots of questions about everyone's ages. So he would ask, 'Is grandfather older than Daddy?' or 'Who is older, Daddy or Grandma?'

Children need to be able to reason about and understand abstract concepts before they can truly understand the cycle of life. Around the age of five a significant shift occurs in the way that children think. For the first time, they become able to look beyond what they can see immediately in front of them and instead focus on other non-observable characteristics.

If two brothers, aged three and five, have been told that they can have a dog as long as it's a small one, for example, the three year old will assume that the black and white spotty puppy he sees at the pet shop is a good choice, because he is small. His five-year-old brother, however, will try to explain that Dalmatian puppies grow into very big dogs. The three year old will not understand this and may keep insisting that the puppy is small; the five year old can see a small puppy in front of him, but is also able to think about the large dog it will become.

Coupled with a developing sense of time, children now have a basic understanding that living things grow and change. Some of the more complex life cycle changes that occur may still confuse them, however, such as the transformation from caterpillar to butterfly or moth. They may assume, for example, that when caterpillars metamorphose into butterflies, they crawl away and butterflies fly in to take their place. Young children are often fascinated by changes like this, even though they do not really understand the process:

Jack, five, loved watching frog spawn turn into tadpoles and then into frogs.

Fabian, five, is constantly finding caterpillars which we keep until they turn into moths. We haven't had a butterfly yet.

At this stage of development, children recognise the difference between animate and inanimate entities without having to rely on the obvious external features they can see, such as breathing and movement. They

By age six children know whether most things are living or non-living, but some – like water – can still be confusing

know that living things share a hidden essence that remains unchanged, despite outward appearances, and that all living animals and plants grow, reproduce and require food and water to survive. They also understand that non-living things such as spinning tops, crystals, clouds and smoke cannot grow in a biological sense and can distinguish between things which are living or dead:

> Jack, five, knows simple examples of what things are living and what are not. He knows if a bug or plant is dead or alive.

The level of knowledge children have about sex still depends entirely on what they have read or are told. When asked about sex, the response from a five year old may vary from a vague idea to a full blow-by-blow account, although the meaning behind the words is still obscure. The following quotations are lovely examples of children's varied levels of understanding at this age:

> Jack, five, knows that he was once a baby and that babies come from their mothers' tummies, but he's never enquired where they come from before that. He knows that other children have brothers and sisters but I don't think he realises that most families normally only have a couple of children because the other day he said, 'I want thirty-nine sisters, forty-eleven brothers and two more babies like Holly.'

> Theo, five, says a baby 'starts off inside your body like a brain or something. Then it grows like a person but it's naked. It comes out of your space hole. It's asleep in your tummy and you have a fat belly.'

> Fabian, five, has been told about the facts of life because when I was pregnant with Maxim he kept asking me how the baby got into my tummy. He just wasn't satisfied with 'Daddy put his seed in Mummy's egg'. He kept saying, 'Yes, but HOW?!' So in the end I explained the whole thing. A few months ago he said to me, 'Mummy, you know that thing you have to do to get a baby in your tummy? Could you please do it tonight because I want another baby.'

Eleanor, five, knows that a baby is made from half a seed from a daddy, and half from a mummy.

When I asked Kishori, five, about sex, she said, 'It's when a man sticks his willy into a girl's winnie, isn't it?' She also sounds very knowledgeable about sperms and eggs and babies. She knows more than many adolescents!

Working things out

By the age of six to seven, children have started to develop theories about how the world works and their ability to think in abstract terms is becoming increasingly sophisticated. Children now have a reasonable understanding of more difficult concepts involving time and have gone beyond the 'now' and the 'not now', so that words such as past, present and future take on new meanings. They begin to understand that days can be broken down into units of time or added together to form larger units, and they soon have sufficient reasoning abilities to use clocks as a reference point for short periods (seconds, minutes, hours) and calendars as a reference point for longer periods (days, weeks, months, seasons and years).

Children can now track the way time passes therefore, and can understand simple concepts of family ancestry and cultural history – for example, they now appreciate that the dinosaurs died out long before Granny was born! Children are still grappling with some of the finer temporal distinctions, however, especially when it comes to working out exactly how long a given length of time is:

The children all know about past and future but precise length of time is difficult – 'How long is a month?', 'When is my birthday?' They find it hard to understand how Holly, seven, can be older if five-year-old Theo's birthday comes first.

Fabian, five, often asks me what comes first, Christmas or his birthday.

By around seven years of age, children can also give biological explanations for reproduction, birth and death. They now appreciate that life is dependent on food, water and the inner (non-observable) workings of the body, and that death occurs when these cease to work. They are also usually fully conversant with the fact that only women have babies and that this ability is a crucial part of what makes a female different from a male. Even so, children see this gender difference in terms of biological fact rather than sexuality and have little concept of the physical or emotional mechanics involved in making love. At this stage, they often find the connection between sex and birth highly amusing or possibly embarrassing:

> Kathy, seven, goes into fits of giggles if you ask her where babies come from. She knows (I told her), but she says, 'It's rude!'

> Anmika, seven, has a fairly clear understanding of the facts of life, but won't talk about it because of embarrassment. She knows it is done by teenagers and grown-ups and starts with kissing! She knows that willy goes into 'winnie' and ends with having babies.

How much children of this age understand about the reproductive process still reflects the level of information they have been given. The following quotations are therefore quite diverse, as is typical of this age group.

> Amanda, six, thinks sex is about kissing and cuddling, getting undressed and touching everybody's private parts.

> Craig, six, and Evan, eight, understand that sex occurs between two people who love each other and that they can make babies . . . Kissing, touching if both want it. That it's private and special. Not very much more.

> Anna, six, and twins Sophie and Jamie, eight, understand about the mechanics and results of sex, and the love, but not the frequency.

Holly, seven, said, 'Men give women eggs by going close to them and then they hatch out. It starts like a big blob. It grows for two or three weeks then it's ready to come out. It comes out of your space [vagina].' When I asked her what sex was she said, 'When you're in love and you dance in front of your boyfriend.' I asked her 'What's love?' and she said, 'When you kiss'.

Children may, however, struggle to understand the relationships of adults around them. For example:

Khalil's father's second wife (I was wife number one) is now married to his uncle (father's brother). He recently asked his uncle, 'Do you and Aunt sleep in the same bed? Do you and Aunt love each other? When will you be getting a divorce? Mummy and Daddy loved each other and are now divorced? Daddy and Aunt loved each other and are now divorced?' He was clearly trying to work out the relationships at present, which admittedly are very complex.

As children learn more about biology at school, they realise that we all have internal body organs, such as the heart, stomach and brain, whose workings are vital for life and good health. Their reasoning powers have now increased sufficiently for them to start understanding that life is dependent on complicated underlying biological processes. This helps them understand the life cycle more deeply and to understand that when these organs stop working properly illness and death can occur, although they may not be entirely clear on the details. For example:

I asked Holly, seven, what happens when you die and Holly said, 'Your brain comes out and all your blood and skin comes off and all that is left is a skeleton.' (We are not a religious family.)

Corey, seven, thinks you have to be about 100 to die, or really ill, or in a terrible accident. He is fascinated by news reports about murdered children, etc. He asks lots of questions about how they died, was there blood. He hasn't had personal experience of death.

As they come to understand the human life cycle, the concept which children take longest to grasp is death . . . hardly surprising, as even adults can find it a difficult concept to come to terms with or a distressing subject to talk about. The issue is therefore easily put to one side and skirted around. This may, in turn, increase children's anxiety and fear about death.

Intellectually, however, children have reached a stage where they can think more abstract thoughts. Worries about death – especially of losing those they love – can now make them quite anxious, but this may depend on their own personal experience (or lack thereof).

Rory, seven, knows intellectually that one day he will die. I think he is probably more fascinated than frightened by the concept of death because he has yet to experience the death of someone he knows.

Georgie, seven, says he is scared at the thought of death.

Khalil, seven, knows that death means loss, sadness, permanent separation. He has speculated about the death of myself and his father and asked, 'Who will look after me?' He does not want me to be cremated – he wants to bury me so he can visit my grave. He likes to explore with me my experience of the death of my mother (his grandmother) as I was only sixteen when she died. He does not appear frightened by death. He has asked if God is a man or a woman.

Taffy, eight, had tears and panic this very evening as the concept of death and the fact that one day she will die suddenly hit her. She was inconsolable and very anxious and we spent a long time discussing the matter. What she couldn't comprehend was the finality of it all. She kept saying, 'Yes but what do you do when you are dead? How do you feel? What do you think? How do you talk?' Absolutely heartbreaking. Any mention of Heaven, reincarnation, etc., didn't have the comforting effect I had hoped for.

Taking a longer view of life and time

By the age of eight, children have a more precise understanding of the passage of time. They are now able to classify past and future events in the order they occurred and are increasingly able to understand time-related concepts. As their abstract thought capacity increases, they can also think more clearly about their own futures and make long-term plans, as noted in Chapter 4.

Many children now enjoy setting up their own time capsules containing photographs, mementoes and favourite things to bury in the garden for posterity. Although making a time capsule is just a game, children's activity and conversation when creating their capsule will reflect their knowledge that one day they themselves will die and their understanding that their photographs and mementoes will be discovered by future generations.

Children of this age also have a solid understanding of the human life cycle, including death and sex, although the nuances of love still escape them. They will not gain a proper understanding of this aspect of human reproduction until adolescence, when the hormone changes of puberty kick in and they start feeling emotions akin to love for themselves. Indeed, during middle to late childhood, many children are embarrassed or disinterested when the mechanics of sex, kissing and love are discussed or seen on TV, as the following quotations suggest:

> When loves scenes come on the TV, Anmika, seven, covers her eyes and says, 'Yuk'. Finds them embarrassing.

> If Taffy, eight, sees someone kissing on TV, she gets embarrassed and turns away, usually exclaiming, 'Yyyuuuuccccckkk!' She and her friend Max (who is more like a brother to her) recently witnessed a couple kissing in Regent's Park and made vomit noises with their fingers in their mouths (not loudly, I stress).

Jordan, eight, does not like watching girly programmes or adverts. If a sex scene comes on TV, he will turn the channel over and usually says, 'Oh brother!' He has no interest in the opposite sex.

Jonathan, nine, is not interested in sex and has never talked to me about it. I suspect that he has little understanding about it. He thinks love scenes on TV are 'silly' and will, on occasion, stop watching from that point.

Mary, nine, seems mildly revolted by the idea of boys in general. Also, kissing scenes on TV produce loud gagging noises from her.

Victoria, ten, understands that sex is how a male and female show their love for each other. She doesn't like to watch love scenes on TV, so she just closes her eyes.

Other aspects of life are well understood, however, including the passage of time. Children now know that time 'flows' and that units of time are consistent intervals, independent of any activity that occurs within them. They can catalogue past events, depending on how recently they have occurred, and can think about more specific time-related concepts like 'next July' or 'last spring'. This may encourage them to keep track of their past experiences by keeping a diary and to plan their future days and personal goals, for example:

Jonathan, nine, extensively plans his football commitments, knowing when each team is playing and whether he can watch it on the TV or listen on the radio.

Twins Tsehai and Amalia, nine, both plan for university, work, bigger houses, birthdays or any gift-receiving time, holidays in the sun, friends, being allowed to go to clubs, wearing make-up in the street, having a dog. Both keep diaries but they may miss out chunks of their year here and there.

Amalia and Tsehai think it hilarious when they see a couple kissing

One of nine-year-old Mary's catch phrases is, 'I can't wait for . . .' and she starts her countdown a couple of months before the day in question.

Christopher, ten, plans for buying a nice house (when grown up). Is forever thinking of ways to make money so that he can buy a house when he grows up. He also counts the days to events.

Older children are often more pragmatic about life, sex and death in general, as they are comfortable with their understanding of the way the world works, are increasingly independent and are developing good self-esteem. Rather than worrying about life and death, they may focus on the practicalities, for example:

Christopher, ten: 'When do you write a will?'
Daddy: 'Usually when you get married or buy a house or have children.'
Christopher: 'Have you written a will?'
Daddy: 'Yes.'
Christopher: 'If you died who would get your things?'
Daddy: 'Mummy.'
Christopher: 'Who would get them if she died as well?'
Daddy (getting worried): 'You and Nicola.'
Christopher: 'Who would look after us if you died?'
Nicola, six: 'Granny and Grandfather.'
Christopher: 'What would we do if you both died?'
Nicola: 'Would we have to walk to Granny and Grandfather's house?'
Christopher: 'No, silly. I didn't mean like that.'

Aisha, ten, knows that people can die from diseases, etc., and when your body can't take any more it switches off. She knows she will eventually die – maybe in sixty years' time. If someone tried to kill her then she would be frightened, but if it happened during her sleep it wouldn't worry her because you wouldn't know.

Christopher, ten: 'I think people shouldn't kill animals.'
Daddy: 'Suppose a tiger was attacking you, would you want me to shoot the tiger?'
Christopher (after a long pause): 'I'm not sure. Someone would die either way.'

This self-assurance about life is often undermined by adolescence, which brings with it sweeping changes such that children may no longer feel in control of their own bodies or their emotions. In boys, testosterone levels start to rise between the ages of eleven and thirteen, which triggers profound changes in body shape, distribution of body hair, voice pitch, skin oiliness and height. In girls, hormone changes tend to start earlier, around the ages of eight or nine, when height and body fat distribution changes and breast buds start to develop. The average age for onset of menstruation is around thirteen, although periods starting anywhere between the ages of ten to sixteen are considered normal.

Many of these signs of puberty are visible to others, which can cause a great deal of embarrassment – especially if children perceive that they are developing faster or slower than their peers. Despite this, these changes all help to underline the human life cycle – especially the issues of growth and reproduction. Adolescence can be a time of great angst, but it is also one of great excitement, as children gain increasing independence and realise the wonders that await them in the adult world which is rapidly approaching. They now have a full understanding of the human life cycle. The enormity of life and the universe has started to sink in and they will soon be in a position to make the most of their own lives and the times in which they are living.

chapter six

state of independence

how many decisions do you make every day? As adults, most of us are capable of living totally independent lives and we make hundreds, even thousands, of decisions every day. These vary in complexity from minor decisions that map out the coming day to major ones that shape – or reshape – our whole lives. Some choices are imposed on us – we may be expected to work certain hours and to obey certain laws and regulations, for example – but even so, the decision to follow these rules or to face the consequences of not doing so remains entirely ours.

During a typical day we have to decide, for ourselves, what time to get up, what clothes to wear, what food to eat, who to see, where to go and even the form of transport we use. After making hundreds of similar decisions during the day, we then decide what to eat in the evening, what programmes to watch (or not watch) on television, which friends to phone (or not phone), what to do (or not do) about the house and when to retire to bed. The decisions don't even end there – we still have to choose whether or not to have a bath, clean our teeth, what nightwear to put on and whether to set the alarm clock. Of course, many of these tasks are done without conscious thought – we are all creatures of habit. Nonetheless, our ability to look after ourselves and make our own decisions is a key factor in our independence.

Larger, life-shaping choices are fewer and often far between, but at some time or other most of us will have to face decisions such as where to live, whom to live with, whether to have children and, if so, how many, and

From helpless babies to adventurous young adults – the transition towards independence is natural for all children

what career to follow. Our independence gives us the power to make such decisions, even though they are not always easy to make. Independence is perhaps a double-edged sword, bringing with it both the freedom to choose and the agony of indecision. Being independent allows us to do what we want to do, in our own way, but at the same time it requires us to take responsibility for our actions . . . an essential part of being human.

Gaining independence is a slow process, however. As children we start off totally dependent on those who care for us, and humans take much longer to reach a state of independence than any other species on Earth. A typical Western child is not ready to leave home until at least their mid to late teens, although in some cultures independence is achieved a few years earlier. Before they can become independent, children must develop a sense of self, learn to take care of themselves, develop and practise the many skills they will need in the adult world, and learn the rules that govern adult behaviour. At the same time, they must learn self control, develop their moral sensibility and discover the need for personal responsibility. The road to independence is not an easy one!

The first steps to independence

We all have a sense of self and individuality that is an integral part of our ability to live independent lives. As described in Chapter 1, however, babies are not born with this sense of self and seem to believe that everyone is part of them and they are part of everyone else. The first vital step along the road to independence is for babies to recognise that they are individuals, separate from everyone else.

A sense of self starts to develop quite early, long before children can speak, and is usually evident by the age of six to nine months when babies no longer cry just because another infant is upset – for the first time, they are starting to act in an independent way.

During the first months of their lives, babies learn an astonishing amount about the people and objects they see around them. They rapidly start to recognise which items or people are familiar and which are not,

Babies' natural wariness is essential for their well-being

and by around six months of age are developing strong emotional bonds with the people who love them and regularly care for them – mothers, fathers and perhaps grandparents, older siblings or a childminder. From about this age, infants start to show a new type of behaviour – that of wariness or fear – towards strangers. They may even cry when an unfamiliar adult approaches:

> When Sapphire, eight months, was approached by a lady she hadn't seen for some time, she hid her head and almost looked shy. When the lady approached her again, Sapphire burst into tears. Her twin, Roman, didn't cry but had a very wary look on his face.

This wariness, or 'stranger anxiety', becomes incredibly important once infants gain mobility and start venturing out to explore their immediate world. As they move around, whether by rolling, crawling, cruising the furniture or toddling, infants move away from the safety of watchful adults, but they do not yet have the experience to recognise which situations are potentially dangerous and which are not. In-built wariness of all new things – including height, darkness, strangers, unfamiliar places and certain animals – is a survival instinct that helps to protect infants until they can recognise those things that are harmful and those that are not. Mobility brings with it increasing independence; the rise of wariness at the same time provides a safety net.

Children vary considerably in the amount of wariness they show. Whether very cautious or virtually fearless however, they all rely heavily on adults at this early stage in their quest for independence. In particular, children look to adults for clues about how to behave in new situations or when faced with an unfamiliar object. In such a situation, young children will watch the responses of their care-givers and look for a variety of verbal and non-verbal clues, such as tone of voice, facial expression and whether the adult moves towards or away from each new object, person or place. If adults seem comfortable, children will join in or explore the new objects themselves; if adults show concern or fear, children are more likely to avoid or back away from the situation or object. But even when assessing someone or something as harmless, children will keep looking back at their carers to check that the situation remains safe:

> At his first 'real' Christmas, when Oliver was about sixteen months, he happily pulled the paper off his presents. Once they were open though, he was uncertain, and needed encouragement from us to play with them – once we played with the toys, he did too.

> Rianna, two, will watch my face carefully when we meet up with friends we haven't seen for a while. If we go to a new park or toddler group, she'll join in after a while, but keeps glancing back at me until she's found her feet.

Interestingly, girls will pick up an adult's fear and move away from a suspicious object more quickly than baby boys. Care-givers seem to know this instinctively and will tend to make more fearful facial expressions

The world can be a frightening place when you are two

when trying to communicate concerns to boys than when they're interacting with girls. As well as looking to their carer for cues, most two year olds are clingy when they are uncertain and will stay close to their care-giver in unfamiliar situations, or if they are wary for any reason:

> Aoífe, two, stays close to me near the road, in a crowd and if a cat or dog is around.

> Louie, two, stays close to me when it's dark.

In more familiar situations, two year olds are braver. When they feel completely comfortable with the situation they are in and the people they are around, they will often start to venture out on their own:

> Oliver, two, is very confident and outgoing if he knows somewhere well. He'll now rush off at toddler group or our local play centre without a second glance.

> Aoífe, two, is very independent at the playgroup.

Toddlers have to cope with learning many new physical, mental and emotional skills at the same time, and acquiring a sense of self goes hand-in-hand with developing an individual personality, learning how to behave socially and learning to talk. By eighteen months of age children have a sense of self that is sufficiently developed for them to recognise their own images in a mirror, and by the age of two most children can recognise themselves in a photograph. Children's growing sense of self is highlighted in their possessive behaviour towards items they feel they own and in their early use of their own names and words such as 'mine', 'me' and even 'I', as is clearly demonstrated by these toddlers:

> At a recent party all the children got presents but Helena, two, took others that she preferred and said, 'This is mine, because I like it.'

> When Dominic, two, is asked, 'Are you a boy or a girl?' he always shouts, 'I am DOMINIC!'

Do it myself

As young children start to realise that they are individuals and can do things in their own right, they start refusing adult assistance and insist on doing some tasks themselves – although with varying degrees of success! For example:

> Natasha, twenty-one months, insists on feeding herself, especially baked beans and what a mess she makes! She refuses help to be fed.

> As a young baby, Helena hated to be fed. She decided at twenty months old that she didn't wear nappies any more and just refused to wear them. She was completely dry day and night a week later! Now she is two, Helena has to do everything for herself. She insists on choosing her own clothes to wear, and putting them on by herself. The only thing she is reluctant to do for herself is the tidying up!

Even at this young age, children take great pleasure in their achievements, however simple these may be. They rapidly expand their repertoire of skills and are often quite firm in refusing adult help when they realise that the mastery of certain tasks is within their grasp:

> Aoífe, two, insists on putting on her shoes, coat, etc., and brushing her teeth herself. She also refuses offers of help with eating.

> James, two, insists on doing virtually everything himself – going up and down stairs, turning on the TV, putting food on his plate, putting his coat and boots on . . . it can take AGES to get out of the house in the morning because he also takes his own time doing everything.

> Maxim, two, insists on getting in and out of the car by himself and will rarely let me feed him.

> Jashan, two, likes to go to the loo alone and, if allowed, would wash himself, clean his own teeth and do all the cooking!

Children's desire to 'do it myself' at this age reflects the beginning of autonomy – as their sense of self develops, so too does the realisation that they have a degree of control over their world. Ultimately, children will become self-governing individuals, but for now it is enough of a challenge to put their boots on by themselves or make an attempt at cleaning their own teeth. This can be frustrating for parents and carers (especially when they are in a hurry) but it is an important stage in young children's development. Mastering simple tasks like those described in the examples above not only provides children with new skills, but also builds self confidence and fosters a sense of independence – both of which will be needed in the years to come.

As their personality and self awareness develops, children of this age also start to show personal preferences for certain colours, toys and playmates. Forming these likes and dislikes is an important way of expressing their individuality and the way they feel about themselves. This is often seen very clearly as children begin to choose the clothes they wear:

Maxim, two, has certain clothes that he loves and that he wants to wear again and again – usually because they have animals on them. He's very keen on looking smart and will run off to show his dad and brother if he's wearing something he particularly likes.

James, two, always wants to wear his wellington boots whatever the weather and wherever he is. They're 'Bob the Builder' wellies and James loves them!

Children's choice of clothes at this age may not always be appropriate of course, and they can get quite upset when forced to wear clothes they do not like for reasons they do not understand.

Aaron, two, wants to wear the same few things and is stubborn although he seems to understand if something is dirty or wet. He likes to choose his own things but doesn't understand about seasonal wear!

Rio, fifteen months, is determined to feed himself

> Jashan, two, will fight over clothes and I generally lose the battles. He
> flatly refuses to wear certain things so I tend just to give in within reason.

Early battles over what to wear are a sign of young children's growing independence, however. At this age, children have a strong enough sense of self to want to have their own way and express their personal preferences. At the same time, however, they lack the mind-reading ability that would allow them to consider anyone else's opinion and do not have enough self control to cope easily with having their desires thwarted.

Temper temper

Two year olds' emerging independence and limited self control are often evident in tantrums. This can be a difficult stage, as children's growing sense of self is accompanied by an increasing sense of anger. Not all children have tantrums, but on the whole tantrums are so common in two year olds that this stage of development is often referred to as the 'terrible twos'.

> Jessica, two, is right in the middle of the 'terrible twos' and will throw
> a tantrum when told not to do something. Even if that something
> would hurt her by doing it.

> Helena, two, has tantrums over clothes.

Tantrums usually occur when children's desires are thwarted and the new-found power accompanying their growing desire for independence is blocked. Frustration quickly builds up when they are stopped from doing something they desperately want to do, or when they do not have the ability to achieve their goals (such as building a higher brick tower, or reaching an object on a high shelf), or when they lack the linguistic skills necessary to make others understand what they need. As children do not yet have a concept of time, frustration can also build up as a result of delays – toddlers live in the here and now and everything must happen almost instantly. Children of this age do not know how to handle the frustration they feel in these

Frustrated desires often lead to tears at the age of two

situations, however, so they react in the only way they can and express their feelings by stamping their feet, hitting out, biting, or flouncing to the floor:

> On a bad day, Jashan, two, will battle about almost anything, for example, 'I don't want to go out with Daddy' then, after Daddy has left, 'I wanted to go with him'. On good days, little troubles him and he has very few tantrums unless he is tired and given food to eat that he doesn't like or forced to wear clothes he dislikes.

> Dominic, two, will have a tantrum if something doesn't go his way or it is not quick enough.

> Oliver, two, can have a tantrum when he can't manage something he's trying to do. The other day, he was trying to fit pieces of Lego together but couldn't. He got frustrated, hurled the Lego across the room and had a tantrum about it. He also has smaller tantrums when I won't let him do things like go outside in the cold wearing only a tee-shirt, or play with the power drill(!).

Despite the distress tantrums can cause (for carers and children), they are a normal aspect of children's development. Tantrums play an important role in children's early learning. The frustration that leads to tantrums also motivates children to learn, acting as a spur to solve problems and develop their skills in the areas causing frustration. Only then will children overcome the source of their frustration. For example, if a child keeps falling off his tiny starter bike, he will try and try again until he develops the skill needed to ride it properly. This helps him learn that practice and perseverance bring their own rewards. Likewise, the frustration that children feel when they do not get their own way encourages them to develop self control and to learn to negotiate for what they want.

Even when a child is not throwing a tantrum, conflicts in which young children protest at the things expected of them, resist requests or repeatedly do what is expressly forbidden occur twice as often at the age of two than just six months previously. Children can seem naughty, disobedient, wilful and contrary and their favourite words may be negative, such as 'no', 'not' or 'won't'. Although difficult to cope with, this also reflects children's developing independence. Having discovered their own will, young children want to exercise it.

At this stage, however, children have no sense of personal responsibility; they are only just beginning to grasp a variety of social rules and need to test the boundaries of what is acceptable behaviour and what is not. In many disputes, young children will often smile or even laugh – almost as if they are deliberately upsetting people to see what reaction this provokes. This is all part of the learning process, however, and is a vital way of testing which rules are consistent and which are applied in a more flexible manner.

Oliver, two, will sometimes catch my eye and then deliberately do something I've just told him not to. He'll smile mischievously while he does it, still looking at me – obviously testing to see how far he can go.

James, two, will sometimes do naughty things on purpose, laughing gleefully despite getting told off.

As children's dexterity and linguistic skills improve, they get more competent at their old challenges and become fascinated by new things which, although difficult and frustrating at first, become increasingly easy to overcome. Achieving new levels of competence boosts children's sense of achievement and independence and at the same time reduces their sense of anger and frustration. As a result, the frequency of temper tantrums gradually subsides and they occur only on certain occasions, such as when children feel tired, bored, threatened or unfairly thwarted:

Rebekah, three, is shy and wary of strangers – she gets angry if I'm talking too long to them and throws a tantrum. She wants their attention but panics when they direct a gaze or question at her and sometimes actually screams and puts her head down to avoid eye contact. If another child at nursery takes her toy away, Rebekah shrieks very loudly and may throw herself on the floor, rolling around.

Zoe and Josh are enjoying new levels of independence

Abigail, three, will have a tantrum whenever she doesn't get her own way, for example, when she doesn't want to walk, when she wants to be picked up, when she wants to watch a video or when she wants sweets.

Standing on their own two feet

By three years of age, children's self control is developing. Children become increasingly able to regulate their own emotions and behaviour. As described in Chapter 4, children are now becoming able to represent the world mentally and think symbolically. Memory is improving, along with language skills. These developments mean that children are now able to express themselves more clearly and are becoming better at solving every-day problems. Frustration and tantrums are now subsiding, although they are unlikely to disappear overnight.

Three year olds also have a firmer sense of self, and are beginning to master a number of important every-day skills such as how to wash and dress themselves. Although they cannot manage many of these skills on their own yet, they are becoming much less dependent on their caregivers and will commonly refuse help even when they are struggling. Having tasted the power of independence, they are now actively striving for more.

Amy, three, refuses to hold my hand inside the nursery school gate.

When shopping at a DIY shop or supermarket, Rebekah, three, likes to run to the bottom of the aisle, up the other and find me again, much to my consternation. At the park, she'll go ahead to the swings.

Many children are attending nurseries or playgroups by this age and this is another arena in which three to four year olds' growing independence is often obvious. Children of this age are generally able to cope remarkably well with short periods away from home, even if they have not been used to day-care previously. They are now able to initiate their own activities and are beginning to enjoy playing in groups of other children.

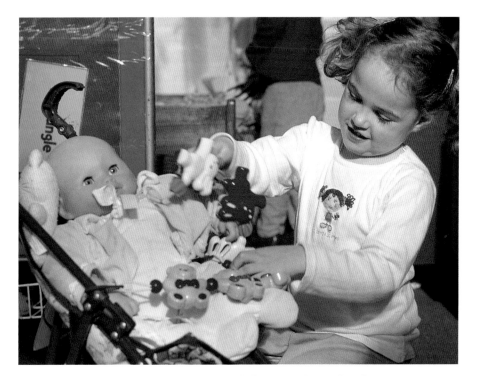

Abigail, age four, treats her doll as an independent being

Children are now becoming aware of their own independence too and beginning to value it. This is evident in many areas of their lives – even in their pretend play. At eighteen months, for example, a child will treat her dolls as dependent human beings which need her help to dress, eat and be told what to do. By the age of three, however, she lets her dolls act independently and express their own desires and emotions, showing the same level of independence as she does herself.

The degree of independence that children are allowed by their carers depends largely on the culture in which they are reared. Children brought up in Europe and the US, for example, learn to be independent, self motivating and to develop their own opinions and goals at a relatively young age. They therefore develop a strong sense of self and of being quite separate from those around them. In contrast, children brought up in cultures that value larger social groups more than the individual develop an identity based on knowing their right place in society, the role that they are destined to play in life, and the duties that are expected of them. They therefore develop a quite different sense of self and a different level of independence based on the good of the community rather than of the individual.

Testing the limits

Whatever culture they are born into, children need to develop both the ability and the desire to behave in ways that their society finds acceptable. They must learn the rules governing acceptable behaviour and also that these rules apply differently in different situations – for example, destructive behaviour that has been banned by adults may be shared with brothers and sisters as long as you do not get caught.

Around the age of four, children start questioning these rules, however, and also learn how to justify their behaviour by shifting the blame. In fact, children often show surprisingly advanced behaviour when they apply their own brand of logic to justify their actions:

> When Saxon, four, didn't want to go to sleep and was told off for reading after lights out, he said he really wanted to go to sleep but his eyes wouldn't let him.

As care-givers keep reminding children of the rules they have broken and explain how their misdeeds make other people feel, children learn the boundaries that apply in the society in which they are growing up. As their growing sense of independence allows them to feel more in control of their own lives, however, they may come into conflict with their carers. Four year olds still have a few tantrums when not getting their own way:

> Leon, four, will have a tantrum if he wants lemonade or chocolate and we say no.

> Akira, four, has tantrums when he doesn't get his own way and there is another adult present, when he doesn't write something well or can't do something.

> Bradley, four, is quite sensitive and is easily upset and frustrated by the things Amanda, six, says and does. He will have tantrums when not getting his own way. Mostly when Amanda annoys him and he doesn't know what to do in that situation, he'll scream and cry.

While testing the limits of their independence, children will often do something they know is naughty, as described in Chapter 2. However, this helps children to define which rules they absolutely must follow and which may be acceptable to break in certain circumstances. Typical examples of early rule breaking include deliberate swearing and using other normally taboo words:

Saxon, four, usually says 'Bother' if something happens that doesn't please him. Recently, when he was told to turn off 'Animal Planet' to go to bed, he said, 'Bother, bother, bother . . . ' then looked me straight in the eye and said, 'Bugger'. I told him it wasn't a nice word to use and he instantly said, 'Bugger, bugger, bugger' with a big grin on his face. Eventually he promised not to say it again and went off to bed saying 'Bother' instead. When he closed his bedroom door, I heard a defiant string of 'Buggers' through the listening monitor. He was mortified when he realised I had overheard him and hasn't used the word since.

The children only use rude words like 'bottom'. They were in the back of the car with a friend the other day and I could hear them all giggling. One of them said, 'I know the "F" word . . . "fart"' and they all roared with laughter.

The onset of 'bad' behaviour such as swearing also shows that children's peers are starting to influence their behaviour. While children have spent most of their time with family members, the rules they have followed and their sense of self has remained fairly constant. When they start spending more and more time at school, however, they learn that other types of behaviour can occur and may start to experiment to see which of these new behaviours (and words) are acceptable at home and which are not. Often this is done in a jokey, testing manner, for example:

Jack, five, jokes about things that he pretends to do, then will say, 'Just joking'. And if Mommy is not happy, he will say, 'Bad joke, huh Mom?'

The self-conscious self

As children reach the age of four and develop the ability to mind read, they take another important step along the road to independence. As explained in Chapter 1, at around the age of four children begin to understand that thoughts, feelings and beliefs underlie people's behaviour. Once they can mind read, children begin to gain a better understanding of people, begin to better appreciate how their own actions affect others and realise that different people have different thoughts, opinions, likes and dislikes.

Coupled with their rapidly developing language and memory skills, children's ability to understand the link between what people think and what they do means that they now begin to understand that they, as independent beings, can influence other people. Four year olds who have made this link soon discover how to use it to their own advantage – for example, instead of losing their temper immediately when thwarted, four year olds will often try to negotiate, sometimes making impressive efforts to cajole, persuade or even directly manipulate others when they want something:

> When Fiona was about four, she discovered the fine art of persuasion and has been practising it ever since. If she wants something, she will say nice things to you, offer to help with whatever you're doing and put on her sweetest smile!

Mind reading enables children to interact with others more successfully and also helps them to recognise not only their own independence but that of other people too. With the realisation that people have different opinions, however, comes another revelation, just as profound: not only do you have opinions about other people, but they also have opinions about you – which may differ somewhat from your own!

This realisation means that children at this age can become extremely self conscious. Some children dislike too much attention because they are shy and easily embarrassed. At this stage, they judge their own worth

Shyness is a natural side-effect of a child's growing awareness that other people hold individual opinions

not only according to their mental and physical prowess, but also on how well they feel they are accepted and understood by family and friends. It can therefore be daunting to feel that everyone is watching their performance and forming an opinion – especially if they think they are being laughed at. Other children thrive on attention and can hardly receive enough, soaking up as much as they can get and even resorting to showing off in an attempt to hold onto the limelight:

Leon, four, is embarrassed at people laughing at him – he gets very angry.

Ellie, five, told me eventually, after a 'performance' for the parents, that she liked ballet but didn't want to go any more because she couldn't stand being looked at. She is acutely self conscious and this stops her doing many things when her parents are around, but apparently when she's not with us she is far more confident and forthcoming. Rosa, three, unlike her older sister, loves to be watched and enjoys an audience.

> Kishori, five, loves to entertain us by dancing (but we mustn't look amused). She is very persistent about things she considers herself good at – generally musical or scholastic things. She fancies herself to be the archetypal 'good girl' and does her utmost to be helpful.

Whether being self conscious or showing off, however, these behaviours show that children are aware that other people have independent minds and opinions. Neither form of behaviour is right or wrong, and whether children are inclined to express themselves freely or behave in a more circumspect manner depends on many factors, including their temperament and the social beliefs of the society that they live in.

School days

The transition to school, around the age of five for most children, is another major landmark on the road to independence. Even children who have not had much experience of being away from home now have to learn to stand on their own two feet. This can be daunting, and the level of independence shown by a five year old can be very variable. Many factors affect how independent children feel at this age – from the familiarity of the situation to their own personality and temperament. Most five year olds will still stay close to their parents or care-givers when in unfamiliar or scary situations:

> Naomi, five, will stay close to me when we are using a lift – she is scared that someone will get left behind.

> Jack, five, will stay close to me if I take him somewhere that he doesn't want to be, for example the doctor, dentist, hospital, etc. He also stays close if there is a big group of kids or a stranger walking towards us. Sometimes if an adult he doesn't know speaks to him he will look at me for encouragement.

Some children, far from being shy, revel in being the centre of attention

At the same time, however, children of this age are increasingly willing to venture out on their own when they are doing something they enjoy and may be happy to move away as long as a familiar face remains in sight. They are starting to want more independence and to take on new responsibilities for themselves, even though they are not yet old enough to go very far on their own.

> If Kishori, five, is with her sister or friends, she may go off and explore, for example at the Natural History Museum.

> Jack, five, loves camping and will wander off at a campsite or at another child's birthday party.

> Fabian, five, loves wandering off down a beach or investigating in a park or playground. He's also quite happy to go off to a friend's house.

Once at school, children's peers play an increasingly important role in their lives. Children now spend more time with their peers, which is both a cause and an effect of their developing independence. Adults also now recognise children's increased ability to think and act for themselves and so allow their children more freedom.

Ultimately, being independent means being able to rely on oneself rather than on parents for support, guidance and decision making, but peers and friends are very important in making this transition. As children grow older, they rely increasingly on their friends; from school age onwards they typically spend more than 40 per cent of their waking hours with their friends. Around this time, as they begin to rely less upon their parents, children can become less willing to share the events of their day with their parents or carers at home, doling out information on a 'need to know' basis only, in true secret service fashion:

> Jack, five, takes after his dad by never talking about his day beforehand, or telling you about it after. Jack's answer to everything is usually, 'Yes, all right'.

Fabian, five, tells me a bit about his day when I ask, but a lot more comes out in dribs and drabs later.

Kishori, five, is moderately forthcoming about her day. She tells me a small proportion of what has happened – usually what she thinks I'm interested in, for example, who wasn't nice to her in the playground, what she had for lunch. She is sparing with details of her work but can chat about exciting events, for example, dressing up as a snowflake for the Christmas play.

Alex, six, is not very forthcoming about his day at the time, but may be a day or so later. He seems to need to process it.

Children's reticence with information reflects their increasing independence and also a developing need for privacy. They are now beginning to understand themselves in increasingly psychological ways, as their capacity for abstract thought develops (described in Chapter 4) – that is, they are becoming able to understand themselves in terms of abstract personality traits, such as shyness or sociability.

Up until this point in their lives, children have tended to judge their own worth mostly according to the feedback they receive from their families and close friends. From now on, however, children's sense of self is increasingly based upon their relationships with their peers, as well as their performance in school and in sport. Once children start spending more time with their peers, they have to follow new rules appropriate for these new social groups, and they start forming new impressions of their own identity as they re-evaluate themselves in the light of their peers' reactions and responses to them. As a result they may start to express and emphasise their individuality in a number of different ways. For example:

Jack, five, expresses his individuality by not doing something that he doesn't want to do even if a big group of children are doing it. He doesn't like to get his hands messy so he won't eat chocolate or play with glue because he might get some on his fingers.

Alex, six, expresses his individuality through drawings, writing, building things, in the things he does and talks about. He will not conform to fit in. For example, he doesn't play football.

Children also show their individuality in the clothes they choose to wear, as these make a certain statement to the world and contribute towards the first impressions other people form of them – of which children are now increasingly aware.

Fabian, five, went through a stage when he would only wear corduroy trousers and then he wanted shorts with deep pockets (so he could put his Pokémon cards in them). I can't get him to wear anything he doesn't want to.

Nicola, six, is embarrassed if seen in clothes she doesn't like and when she has had her hair cut or put up.

Young school age children are often able to stand up for themselves and others such as friends or siblings. Their own sense of independent power is now significant. Some are more comfortable exerting their independence than others, but most will try to defend themselves if they feel wronged. Children of this age are less easy to persuade to go along with something they do not want than younger children and can sometimes be surprisingly feisty when sticking up for themselves or those they care about, as the following quotations suggest:

Fabian, five, is quiet but strong willed. This week he mistakenly took his Pokémon cards to school. He realised in the car on the way and Theo, seven, tried to convince Fabian to let him, Theo, look after the cards for him. Fabian quickly but firmly said that he wanted my friend Katie, who was driving, to take the cards back home to me. This might not seem such a big deal, but Theo was putting a lot of pressure on Fabian and Katie said she was impressed by how Fabian stood up for himself.

Amanda, six, is a very strong character. She is very caring; if someone starts on her sibling she jumps on top of the situation and takes complete control.

Nicola, six, is pretty assertive, although often just by shouting loudly. At present there is a major conflict with her teacher at school over wearing her hair in a pony tail. Nicola is resolute about not doing this.

Playing by the rules

As well as asserting their own individuality, children now need to learn to co-operate with others, in particular with their peers. Within a peer group, children will seek to establish their own hierarchy in which there is a recognised authority and organisation. Those with a strong sense of independence and more forceful personalities will tend to become leaders, at the centre of their group, while others will be happier as

Aaron hangs out with his gang

followers and will seek to fit in with what everyone else is doing. Both roles are essential for the successful functioning of a peer group and children's roles often vary, depending on the group they are with:

Georgie is a leader when she's clearly the oldest child in the group and in groups of two. In bigger groups of peers she tends to follow.

Whatever their role, as children spend less time under direct adult supervision, they will spend much of their time playing games or 'just hanging around' interacting with each other. The games children play at this age are usually based on strict rules which determine what they can and cannot do. Rule-based games usually involve a number of children and can last much longer than the role-playing fantasy games that were enjoyed earlier in childhood. Prior to the age of six, children will often change the rules of a game at a whim, but now rules are usually agreed in advance and followed consistently. These rules are also strictly adhered to and anyone who changes them without common consent will be accused of cheating. Rules are important to children at this age – and often very complex:

Khalil, seven, constructs inordinately complex rules which no one else can follow.

Rule-based games are actually very important in helping children understand the rules of the society in which they will one day have to act as independent adults. Following the rules and aiming to win helps children to keep pre-established goals in mind and also teaches them how to work both as individuals and as a team. In the structured situation that a rule-based game provides, children can practise balancing their own desires (for example, to win) against the rules of the group. This helps them understand that formal structures apply in society as much as they do in games. Children will even make a simple rule-based game out of a rule-based adult situation. This helps them to understand and

Spending time with peer groups is important for children's self-esteem and identity

Once past the age of six, children increasingly enjoy rule-based games

learn about that particular adult convention, as well as teaching them how to regulate their own behaviour and take a certain amount of responsibility upon themselves. For example:

Nicola, six, and her brother Christopher, ten, will occasionally play a game of trying to be really well behaved and grown up when having a meal with the grandparents.

Game-based interactions also help children develop their understanding of the thoughts, intentions and actions of the other players who are pursuing their own goals. Conflicts occur, but these help children to learn the arts of negotiation, compromise and discussion which are vital for survival in the real world:

Holly, seven, used to fight with me about clothes, but can now see reason. She will understand if I say it doesn't go or it's too hot. Her taste is very different to mine and we have to compromise.

Although they may follow the rules set up by their peers, children's growing sense of independence may make them more rebellious at home, where they are likely to continue testing the rules imposed by their parents.

> Nicola, six, insists on doing almost everything herself, but not tidying her bedroom. She can be rebellious by refusing to wear clothes that her mother has bought. She can also be pretty defiant and will not back down, virtually however cross one is with her.

> Theo, seven, is often rebellious. He always wants to do things his own way. He won't get into the bath and then he won't get out.

> Corey, seven, rebels a lot and will do exactly what you tell him not to i.e., slam a door when I have just said not to. He never rebels at school – in fact he is too good and quiet.

Corey's behaviour, described above, is also very common at this age – children of this age will often respect the rules laid down by authorities other than parents while letting their hair down at home:

> Holly, seven, and Theo, five, seem to operate different boundaries at home and at school. At school they are apparently paragons of virtue. At home, they might pinch or bite each other, but they would never do that kind of thing at school.

> It makes a big impression on Theo, seven, when someone at school is naughty and has to be sent to the headmistress. He would never be naughty at school. He also knows that there are rude words that he must never use at school, but he is quite happy to use them at home.

Children's rebellion at this age often involves the use of swear words, which they know are not allowed, even though they do not necessarily understand what they mean.

> Taffy, eight, said one 'shit' and one 'bloody' on two different occasions in front of, of all people, my mother-in-law. It did not go down well at all.

> Max, seven, has brought home swear words from school and used
> them. He started with the 'F' word and some other swear words with
> sexual connotations. He knows it is wrong to use them and they are
> not tolerated in school or at home. I feel he uses them sometimes
> more like a 'dare' or to be 'cool'.

> Theo, seven, discovered the 'F' word about eighteen months ago and
> used it all the time until, in desperation, I told him what it really
> means. He hardly ever uses it any more!

> Danielle, eight, is just starting to swear at school. I have only heard
> her say 'bloody' once, although recently she asked about the 'F' word.

Children may also now start rejecting certain rules about right and wrong
which have been imposed on them by their parents, especially when they
see these rules being broken by adults, for example:

> Theo, seven, knows there are rules which I think are stupid. For
> example, bicycles aren't allowed in our park, which is very sad for the
> children, and so we let them ride their bikes until the park keepers tell
> them to get off. This summer, we visited a castle in Scotland which
> had a beautiful garden. Unfortunately, there was a 'Keep off the grass'
> sign. I voiced my opinion that it was a stupid rule and Theo walked
> onto the grass. I had to explain that just because I thought it was
> stupid didn't mean he could ignore the rule.

As children get older, however, and more independent, they start to
understand that rules, although essential for the smooth-running of a
group, are somewhat arbitrary. Although they still spend a lot of time
playing rule-based games, they will now adapt and change the rules quite
comfortably – as long as the group democratically agrees to the change.

At the same time, children start to make their own decisions about
morality and behaviour. They are now able to consider more than one
aspect of a given situation at once and are able to compare and contrast
these aspects, as described in Chapter 4. Being able to think in this way

has important implications for moral reasoning and the development of independence: children now start to weigh up several factors simultaneously when making moral judgements and become able to make simple, but informed, choices.

By around eight or nine years of age, children take into account people's differing physical and emotional needs when making moral judgements. They may, for example, feel that someone deserves more of something because they are poor, or because they are feeling sad or are physically disabled – as if trying to recreate equality by weighting things in favour of those who find life most challenging. So while a group of six year olds might decide that everyone gets three swings with the bat in a ball game, regardless of size, ability or any other factor, nine year olds might agree on a handicapping system which allows weaker players an extra go or underarm bowling.

Taking responsibility

To function successfully within their peer group, children have to learn how to behave in an appropriate way towards each other. They have to find the right balance between the positive feelings produced by achieving their personal, independent goals and the negative feelings produced if they act outside accepted boundaries and attract disapproval. Finding this balance helps children learn to take responsibility for their own actions, which is an essential aspect of independence.

Kathryn, six, is well aware of right and wrong and would take responsibility for her own actions.

In the process, children must develop an internal set of standards against which they can assess whether their behaviour is right or wrong, leading to feelings of guilt or pleasure accordingly. Between the ages of seven and eight, children begin to feel complex emotions such as pride, guilt or shame even when the actions leading to the emotion are not witnessed by anyone else. Younger children tend to feel these emotions most strongly

Choices, choices ... By the age of nine, Amalia and Tsehai are able to take responsibility for their own decisions in life

only when their actions are witnessed – and judged – by someone else. Seven and eight year olds now start talking about feeling proud or ashamed of themselves in contrast to younger children who only talk about whether other people feel proud or ashamed of them:

> Holly, seven, often argues and then days later will apologise. She thinks about events afterwards and then will say, 'I behaved badly the other day, didn't I?'

This conscience helps children feel personally responsible for their own actions which, in turn, gives them a greater sense of power and personal freedom. They are now able to learn a duty of responsibility for their actions towards others and are developing increasingly strong opinions about what is right and what is wrong:

> Anmika, seven, told me off for proposing not to collect a friend from school (and letting the mother down).

Rory, seven, makes decorative boxes full of old toys to give as Christmas presents to a charity – he's getting a broader social conscience now.

Twins Amalia and Tsehai, nine, are very upset if I say we'll do something and then I don't. This is like betrayal so for the remainder of the day every issue will return to the fact I 'lied'. Quote from Amalia: 'I thought you said you don't lie, well you're lying now!'

As they develop a sense of personal responsibility, children's ability to govern their own behaviour increases. This can be illustrated by giving children of this age a moral dilemma to solve in which they must choose whether or not to knowingly break an important rule imposed by someone they respect and normally obey.

For example, children are told a story in which they have been given permission by their mother to walk to school on their own, as long as they do not stop along the way. On the way, however, they come across another child needing help. The dilemma is then whether to stop and help, thus breaking their mother's rule. Given this dilemma, younger children generally say that they should follow their mother's instructions and not stop. Older children, however, will say they should stop and help, realising that their mother's orders have been superseded by the new situation. Children who make the latter judgement demonstrate an ability to take responsibility for their own actions and are showing the self-government that characterises adult independence.

How much responsibility any one child can manage varies widely of course, but parents and carers are generally good judges of the degree of independence and responsibility with which their children can be entrusted. By about eight years of age, most children have mastered the basic competencies of caring for themselves, however, including the ability to take care of their own clothes, answer and make phone calls without help, eat unaided, entertain themselves alone and – in some cases – to play outside without supervision, although this will largely depend on where people live and whether or not they have a safe play area.

All the children (aged six to nine) play 'out'. In the past year they have all started to play on the pavement in front of our house with our neighbours' children. There are about twelve children who regularly play together. There are set rules like remaining on the pavement and only playing between numbers 25 and 41 on our road. They love it. We parents are slightly anxious and remain watchful but love the independence and confidence it gives the children. Many of them walk to school together some mornings.

Majenta, eight, occasionally goes to school or the corner shop by herself (five minutes away) but would love to be allowed more independence. She would love to play out in the street and roam around but can't because of safety. She goes on holiday with my parents and stays overnight at her friends' houses without a second thought.

The independent self

As children gain an increased sense of independence, they start moving away from their parents or other care-givers and their relationships with them start to change in a number of ways. Parents tend to show their children fewer obvious signs of affection so the number of hugs and kisses goes down. This probably happens at least partly because children become acutely embarrassed if they are shown affection in public – they see this as being treated 'like a baby' which, with their new-found sense of independence, is the last thing they want.

Taffy, eight, has this thing whereby she tells me her batteries need recharging and she'll hug me until she says, 'Ping! I'm done!' The next minute she's getting cross because I kiss and cuddle her too much. She is embarrassed by me kissing her goodbye at school in the morning and (God forbid) fussing over her or talking about her in front of someone – albeit complimentary stuff.

For similar reasons, children at this age can also get very embarrassed if they are singled out in front of their friends, or if their parents do anything which children feel might show them up:

> Danielle, eight, is embarrassed if her name is called out in class.

> Majenta, eight, gets embarrassed if I tell her off in front of anyone.

> Max, nine, is embarrassed if I sing or dance and is embarrassed by my working at his school.

> Mary, nine, says she is embarrassed at 'My mum shouting swear words at car drivers'.

Socially, children's peer groups also continue to be extremely important to them. As well as providing a bench mark against which to compare themselves, peer groups teach children to value one another. Groups of friends have well-developed internal dynamics by the time children reach eight to nine years of age, and children now regularly compare themselves with others of their own age. By this age, they can assess their abilities in a number of areas, including their emotional, intellectual, social and physical prowess, to form an overall impression of their general self worth with which they will try to impress others.

At first, comparisons are often announced loudly with statements like, 'I can jump higher than you' or 'My drawing is best' but children soon realise that bragging is not socially acceptable and quickly learn to make more subtle comparisons unless they deliberately want to upset another child. Their perceptions of how they measure up play a major role in their sense of identity and self esteem. They become increasingly sensitive to their status among their friends and how they think other people view them.

> Sarah, eight, very much follows the crowd, wanting to do what she feels a grown up girl of eight should do. She does things because they will impress her friends as opposed to expressing her individuality.

Interestingly, from the age of eight onwards, children's assessments of themselves usually match assessments made by their friends and teachers. Children also now start to form a picture in their mind of the sort of person they would like to be – their 'ideal self' against which they will compare what they see as their 'actual self'. If the difference between the two is small it can act as motivation to improve, but if it is large, children can be discouraged and their self esteem may be dented. In their efforts to become more like their 'ideal selves', however, children sometimes go out of their way to please and be nice at this stage. For example:

> Jordan, eight, recently tidied the flat. He's never done this before.

> Jadine, nine, made me breakfast in bed for my birthday.

> Taliesin, nine, compliments me when I dress for work. And when I woke up with back-ache, he massaged my back.

Yet another sign of children's more adult-like sense of independence appears in the way they deal with conflict. They now react more maturely to being thwarted and are less likely to indulge in whining, yelling or hitting if they can't get their own way. Instead, they start to argue with their parents and take great pleasure in pointing out parental errors, white lies and other inconsistencies:

> Sarah, eight, likes to have the last word.

> Majenta, eight, is sometimes rebellious in always wanting the last word and sometimes not knowing when enough is enough.

> Taffy, eight, is quietly assertive. She has a strong sense of self and won't be pushed around easily. She can hold her own on most occasions.

> Mackenzie, nine, will answer back if he thinks I'm wrong.

> Kaspar, nine, keeps telling me not to smoke because it's bad for me. He is going through a pre-teenage phase when I ask him to do things: 'Not fair', 'Don't want to do that', 'That's boring' – lots of negativity.

State of independence

As children approach adolescence, their increasing independence attracts more responsibility and most are now expected to help with chores around the home. Some children even take it upon themselves to do little tasks that they realise need attention, without being asked:

> Jonathan, nine, ran the younger children's bath for me the other day when I was rather pushed for time, without being asked, and got out their pyjamas, etc.

Overall, however, children now increase their separation from their parents. Young adolescents spend twice as much of their free time outside school with their friends as opposed to with adults. Groups of friends enlarge and children's closest friendships become more intimate. Shared trust and loyalty allow the sharing of secrets – which are definitely kept from their parents at this age.

> When I asked Christopher, ten, what kind of secrets he keeps from me, he replied, 'I'm not saying!'

> Rowan, eleven, keeps secret some of what he gets up to, especially things he does that he knows he isn't supposed to.

> Imogen, thirteen, keeps secret the things her friends get up to.

These friendships are important; older children and teenagers define themselves and explore their identities through conversations with friends in which they bare their souls and share their inner thoughts and feelings. Friendships between girls tend to be more intense than those between boys, who tend to form looser relationships among a wider number of friends, but friendship is equally important to both sexes as they begin to break away from their families and truly develop their own identities.

Imogen, thirteen, is now old enough to take responsibility
for keeping an eye on her little sister Aoife

Children are also able to think more deeply about other people's points of view now, and may start to think quite deeply about social issues, morality, politics – usually around the age of fourteen. They will become more aware of the ways in which the behaviour of certain people does not fit into accepted limits and may also become more idealistic and keen to do what they believe is right. Many will be quite forceful when defending their emerging beliefs:

Imogen, thirteen, expresses her individuality by having strong opinions and being single-minded and not afraid to speak out.

The teenage years will not be easy – adolescents are often beset with chronic self doubts and rarely enjoy the conflicts that they are likely to engage in at home any more than their parents. Transgression now becomes a way of life, as teenagers set out to deliberately distance themselves from adults – often breaking as many adult conventions as they can via their clothes, language and attitudes. Ironically, in their efforts to mark themselves out as individual and independent, most teenagers simply align themselves completely with their peer group, but this still represents independence from the parents or carers upon whom they were once utterly dependent.

It is now only a few years until these nearly adult children are capable of totally independent living and making life-shaping decisions such as selecting a career, attending a college or university, or gaining a full-time job. Once they can earn their own living, they may decide to move out of the family home and find their own accommodation. They will become fully functioning, self-governing, independent members of society who have learned how to mind read, mastered the lying game, discovered their gender role, can think for themselves and fully understand the mechanics of the human life cycle. When that happens, children have become adults and have reached their true state of independence.

acknowledgements

Many thanks to all the parents and children who have contributed to this project, including supplying the delightful quotes which helped to make this book so interesting to write, and appealing to read.

The writings, research and ideas of the following people inspired either directly or indirectly both the television series of *A Child's World* and this book. They are most gratefully acknowledged:

M Anderson; J Atkinson; S Atran; C Beal; T Berry Brazelton; S Biddulph; M Boekaerts; E de Bono; M Bowden; T Brazelton; W Bukowski; R Byrne; A Campbell; W Cartwright; P Christensen; M Cole; S Cole; D Crystal; A Cutting; W Damon; R De Vries; M Donaldson; A Douglas; J Dunn; D Einon; N Eisenberg; L Eliot; W Friedman; C Garvey; R Gelman; R Goldman; S Golombok; A Gopnik; U Goswami; C Green; C Greene; S Greenfield; A Harris; P Harris; W Hartup; D Hay; S Hayman; C Hughes; M Hughes; B Inhelder; A James; C Jessel; M Johnson; A Karmiloff-Smith; P Kuhl; D Kuhn; P Leach; R Lewis; J Matter; M Matthews; D Medin; A Meltzoff; W Mischel; V Morrow; J Morton; A Newcomb; J Oates; T Ollendick; D Parke; J Perner; J Piaget; S Pinker; P Pintrich; M Ross; Z Ruben; M Rutter; H Schaffer; M Shatz; R Siegler; E Slater; G Snodgrass; M Stoppard; M Taylor; C Temple; B Tizard; S Turecki; S Ward; H Wellman; A Whiten; H Wimmer; D Winnicott; N Yelland; J Youniss; M Zeidner

index

A

'accidents' and 'mistakes' 42–3, 78
adolescence 206–7, 247–8
affection, shows of 243
age, understanding of 173–4, 195
aggressive behaviour 101, 120
altruistic behaviour 48–9, 50
anger 23
animals 170–2, 192, 194, 196
animism 184
appearance-reality distinction 115–16, 148,
    151, 157
assertiveness 54, 101, 233, 245
attention span 71
autism 16–17
autonomy 217

B

babies and infants
    awareness of life 170
    emotions 23
    exploring the world 133–4, 136
    gender, perception of 95
    learning ability 134, 136, 210
    and mirrors 19–20, 214
    self recognition 20, 23
    sense of self 19, 23, 210–11
    see also newborn babies
biological inheritance 186–7
bossiness 53, 54
boys/girls see gender
brains 98–9, 120
bullying 55

C

cause and effect, awareness of 149, 156
chores, household 247
clothes 109–10, 217–18, 232
cognitive development see thinking
comfort, children's attempts to give 26
communication

making statements 31
and mind reading 16
newborn baby 17, 59–60
talking at and over each other 43–4
see also language
comparing and contrasting 152–5
conflict, dealing with 245
crawling and walking 10
crying-together reflex (contagious crying) 19

D

death, understanding of 190, 192, 194–5,
    201–2, 206
differences in development 10
disgust 23
distance, understanding 146, 152, 159–60, 161
distress, sensitivity to 26, 52
drawing 142–3, 147, 156

E

embarrassment 23, 244
emotions 23, 24, 25, 240–1
    self-conscious emotions 23, 24, 25
    self-consciousness evaluative emotions 24
empathy 26, 42
envy 23
equality and fair play, notions of 52, 90–1,
    128, 240
exploring the world 133–4, 136, 145, 154,
    161, 162, 165

F

fantasising 71, 72, 86
    see also pretence
fear 23, 211
fighting/hitting 70, 79, 80
friendships 8, 28–9
    based on mutual liking and trust 46, 53,
        54, 247
    based on shared activities 46, 54
    falling-out and making up 48

'girlfriends' and 'boyfriends' 189
imaginary friends 35–6
investing in 47
maintaining 53
mind-reading skills and 46–8
opposite-sex friendships 128
pack behaviour 125
same-sex friendships 124, 125, 247
selective friendships 47
and self-esteem 47

G

games
    game-based interactions 237
    rule-based games 234, 239
    see also play
gender 10, 92–129
    babies' perception of 94, 95–6
    brain development and 98–9
    children's understanding of 106–8
    gender constancy, awareness of 94,
      114–15, 116, 118
    gender identity development 98–9, 101,
      117

gender segregation in play 118–20, 122–5
genitals 106–7, 117, 187
learning appropriate gender behaviour
    111–12
misidentification 105
relaxation of gender stereotypes 126–9
role models 111–12, 114, 125–6
societal rules 94
stereotypes and stereotyped behaviour
    96–7, 102, 104–5, 108–12, 114, 125–6
genitals 106–7, 117, 187
good and bad behaviour 62–3, 69
'goody goody' behaviour 82–3
grandparents 194, 195
grooming rituals 112
growth and change, awareness of 172–3,
    183–4, 186, 196
guilt 23–4, 240

H

helping themselves 215, 217
honesty 68
human life cycle 10, 166, 168, 187, 194,
    195–6, 200, 201, 202, 203, 207

I

imaginary friends 35–6
independence 208–48
individuality 17, 18, 27, 28, 210, 217, 218,
    231–2, 233, 248
intellectual realism 156
interacting with others 8, 15, 19, 24, 28–32,
    52, 227
    see also friendships; play
intuition 118, 132, 149, 156

J

joy 23

L

language
    learning 140–2
    linguistic skills 31–2, 43, 147, 221, 222, 226
    in pretend play 35
leaders and followers 54, 233–4
life
    awareness of 168–72, 183–4, 186, 196–7
    living in the present 172–3, 179

see also human life cycle
lying 10, 56–91
    'bad' lies 72, 73
    becoming good at 73–8, 84, 89
    black-and-white thinking 81, 82
    blaming others 66, 68, 84–5
    children's understanding of 72
    deceptive behaviour 63, 64, 68, 73–4, 91
    and fantasy 71, 72, 86
    fibs (trivial lies) 56, 72, 73, 79, 81, 84
    inexperienced liars 74, 76, 77, 84
    and mannerisms 77
    and morality 58, 73
    selective lying 82
    social skill 56, 58, 87, 88
    white lies 8, 56, 72, 73, 79, 81, 87, 88–9, 90

M

make-believe *see* pretence
manipulative behaviour 48, 54, 55, 60, 63, 91,
    227
materialism 46
mathematical and scientific skills 153–4,
    159–160, 161, 162
memory 132, 144, 154–5, 222, 226
    expansion 36, 71, 139, 176
    in newborn babies 94
    short-term memory 36, 162
    storage and recall 159
menstruation 207
mind-reading skills 8, 10, 15–55, 71, 218,
    226, 227
    attainment 41, 44
    'false belief test' 38, 40
    and friendships 46–8
    key skill 36, 38
    mind-reading network 45
    necessity for 16
    negative uses 54–5
    and play 44, 45
    testing for 38, 40
    'theory of mind' 38
    understanding another's intentions 43, 53
    understanding different perspectives 15,
        27, 34, 36, 42, 50, 115–16
misbehaviour, deliberate 70, 136, 225
money, understanding of 153, 159, 160
morality/moral sensibility 8, 58, 70, 79, 80,
    90, 239, 240, 248

black-and-white thinking 80, 81, 84
   development 58, 90–1
   shades of grey 87
music, playing 159

N
nature and nurture 94, 101, 105
newborn babies
   communication 17, 59–60
   facial recognition 19, 94–5, 169
   identification with own species 19
   memory capacity 94
   social development 18–19
   see also babies and infants
nurseries and playgroups 222

P
peer groups 48, 124, 230, 231, 233–4, 240,
   244, 248
personality development 23, 214, 217
perspectives
   self-oriented perspective 28, 68, 79, 147
   understanding different perspectives 15,
     27, 34, 36, 42, 50, 115–16
play
   experimental play 147
   gender segregation in 118–20, 122–5
   gender-inappropriate play 124
   and mind-reading skills 44, 45
   parallel play 30–1
   playing outside 242–3
   pretend play 32, 34–6, 44–6, 71, 137–8, 223
   role play 31, 34–5, 36, 44, 45–6, 55
   sex-stereotyped behaviour 102, 105, 120, 124–5
   see also games; toys
pocket money 153, 160
poetry 142
possessiveness 24, 69, 214

preferences, personal 217–18
pretence 32, 34–6, 44–6, 71, 137–8, 223
   imaginary friends 35–6
   joint pretence 36, 138
   role play 31, 34–5, 36, 44, 45–6, 55
pride 23–4, 240, 241
privacy, need for 231
problem solving 157, 162, 165
puberty 207

R
reasoning 132, 136, 148, 156, 173, 183
   associative reasoning 149
   by analogy 136, 148
responsibility, personal 220, 240, 241, 242
reticence with information 230–1
right and wrong 64, 70, 79, 84, 241
   distinguishing between 62–3, 69, 77, 80,
     91, 240
risk and chance, principles of 161
role play 31, 34–5, 36, 44, 45–6, 55
roles, negotiating for 45
rules
   breaking 225, 234, 248
   rule-based games 234, 239
   testing 70, 136, 220, 238–9

S
sadness 23
school 229
'second order' theory of mind 88
secrets 247
self control 218, 220, 222
self esteem 46–7, 55, 72, 244, 245
self recognition 20, 23
self, sense of 19, 23, 24, 25, 28, 47, 210–11,
   214, 217, 222, 223, 231, 245
self-assessment 245
self-consciousness 227, 229
selfishness/unselfishness 24, 25, 50, 68
sex, understanding of 186–90, 198–9, 200–1,
   203–4
shame 23–4, 240, 241
showing off 227, 229
shyness 231
signs and symbols 139, 140, 142, 143, 146
social development 8, 18–19, 45
socially acceptable behaviour 59, 60, 63, 70,
   78, 79, 87, 136, 224

spatial awareness 146, 147
stealing 78
stranger anxiety 211
surprise 23
swearing and taboo words 70, 225, 238–9

T
taking turns 45
tantrums 218–20, 221–2, 224
telephones, using 27
'terrible twos' 218
testosterone 98, 101, 207
thinking 7–8, 10, 130–65
    abstract thought 139, 149, 158–62, 173,
        178, 203, 231
    comparing and contrasting 152–5
    intuitive thinking 118, 132, 149, 156
    logical thought 147, 151, 152, 161, 162
    symbolic thought 143
    theories, testing 157–8
    thinking ahead 144, 158–9, 203
    see also memory
three-dimensional awareness 147

time
    concept of 173, 174–6, 178–80, 183, 199,
        203, 204
    measurement 166
    telling the 154, 159
time capsules 203
topographical awareness 146, 152
toys
    dolls 96, 184, 223
    possessiveness 24, 25, 69
    sex-stereotyped toys 96–7, 105, 108,
        110
    taking 24, 68, 69
    see also play
trust and loyalty 53, 247
truth 68, 72, 84
twins 19, 204

V
verbal skills see language

W
wariness 211–12, 214, 221, 229